SUSTAINABLE LIVELIHOODS

SUSTAINABLE
LIVELIHOODS

Building on the Wealth of the Poor

KRISTIN HELMORE AND NARESH SINGH

Kumarian
Press, Inc.

Sustainable Livelihoods: Building on the Wealth of the Poor
Published 2001 in the United States of America by Kumarian Press, Inc.,
1294 Blue Hills Avenue, Bloomfield, CT 06002 USA

Copyedit, design, and production by Joan Weber Laflamme, jml ediset, Vienna, Va.
Index by Robert Swanson
Proofread by Philip J. N. Trahan/Sarov Press

Printed in the USA on acid-free paper by Thomson-Shore, Inc.
Text printed with vegetable oil-based ink.

∞ The paper used in this publication meets the minimum requirements of the American National Standard for Information Sciences—Permanence of Paper for Printed Library Materials, ANSI Z39.48–1984.

Library of Congress Cataloging-in-Publication Data

Helmore, Kristin.
    Sustainable livelihoods : building on the wealth of the poor / Kristin Helmore and Naresh Singh.
        p. cm.
    Includes bibliographical references.
    ISBN 1-56549-132-7 (pbk. ; alk. paper)
        1. Economic development. 2. Sustainable development. 3. Human capital. 4. Rural poor—Government policy—Africa—Case studies. 5. Rural development—Government policy—Africa—Case studies. I. Singh, Naresh. II. Title

HD75.H43 2001
362.5'2'091734—dc21

                                                                        2001037689

10 09 08 07 06 05 04 03 02   10 9 8 7 6 5 4 3 2   First Printing 2001

Contents

Acknowledgments

This book was researched and written by Kristin Helmore, an independent journalist. The approach to development described in this book is based on ideas and field work developed and tested by Naresh C. Singh (Principal Adviser, Poverty and Sustainable Livelihoods, Bureau for Development Policy, UNDP) and his colleagues. No such book is of course possible without also drawing on the thoughts and experiences of a number of development practitioners and organizations, as well as on the research and writings of many people in donor agencies, NGOs, universities, and the public and private sectors.

In particular, staff members of the Bureau for Development Policy (BDP) at the United Nations Development Programme (UNDP) have contributed extensively. We would like to thank Paul D. Boyd, Samir S. Wanmali, and Heather Rogers for their editorial support. Heartfelt thanks also go to Eimi Watanabe (Assistant Administrator of UNDP and Director of BDP), Jon Gilman (UNDP Sustainable Livelihoods Unit), Thierry Lemaresquier (Director of UNDP's Social Development and Poverty Elimination Division), Sarah Murison (UNDP's Senior Technical Advisor for Gender and Development), Jorge Zapp, Nancy Golbre, Gillian Hart, and Leonard Joy (UNDP consultants), Jose Garson (UN Capital Development Fund), Jennifer Sebstad (UN International Research and Training Institute for the Advancement of Women), Lalao Ramanarivo (UNDP Assistant Resident Representative, Madagascar), R. H. E. Mapemba (principal economist at the National Economic Council and Coordinator of the Sustainable Livelihoods Programme, Malawi), Stewart Ligomeka (District Development Officer for Mchinji District, Malawi), Peter Kulemeka (UNDP's Assistant Resident Representative and Sustainable Livelihoods Programme Manager, Malawi), Terence Jones (UNDP Resident Representative, Malawi), Peter Jere (core facilitator of the Sustainable Livelihoods Programme at the village level, Malawi), B. T. Costantinos (Team Leader of UNDP's Sustainable Livelihoods Programme, Malawi), Kristine Jones (PAPSL

Advisor to the National Economic Council, Malawi), Dominico Nkhuwa (son of the chief in Nyamawende, Malawi), Phosiso Sola (environmental botanist, Zimbabwe), Ashok Khosla (President of Development Alternatives, India), Gunter Pauli (Director of ZERI), Janis Gravitis (Institute of Advanced Studies, United Nations University, Tokyo), Galina Telysheva, (Latvian State Institute of Wood Chemistry), Richard Stanley (Stanlinks, USA), Anil K. Gupta (SRISTI–Honey Bee network, India), Tekleweyni Assefa (Director of REST, Ethiopia), Haimanot Kebedew (REST client, Ethiopia), and Susan Johnson (ActionAid, UK).

Fieldwork and writing have been made possible through the financial support of UNDP Headquarters and country offices. The opinions and comments in this book do not necessarily reflect the opinions of UNDP or its counterparts.

General and Sustainable Livelihoods Glossary

Language is one of the most important symbol systems in human society. The words that are chosen are the vehicles through which images, attitudes, and values are conveyed, reinforced, and directed. Language suggests philosophies about the culture and the speakers' projected relationship with themselves and their listeners. It is arguable that the reality of a given group is, to a large extent, unconsciously built upon its language habits; we understand and experience very largely as we do because language habits of the field predispose certain choices of interpretation.

Organizations and fields of study inevitably develop their own particular jargon. Jargon inevitably becomes a part of the "knowledge" of the organizations. In other words, jargon represents a guide on how to communicate, sustain, and develop attitudes about a group's institutional knowledge. Therefore, in the interest of "speaking the same language," following are interpretations of meanings and descriptions as they relate to the development field and the concept of Sustainable Livelihoods:

Activities	Designated by work, either in the formal or informal sector
Assets	Designated by human capital, social capital, natural capital, and physical capital
Capability	The characteristic of being capable; the ability to do something*
Consciousness-raising	Rooted in the US women's movement but denoted as the process in which group discussions about personal experiences awaken one's sensitivity to one's own experiences
Development	Good change*

Deprivation	Lacking what is needed for well-being. Deprivation has dimensions that are physical, social, economic, political, and psychological/spiritual. It includes social inferiority, physical weakness, isolation, poverty, vulnerability, powerlessness, and humiliation*
Empowerment	Has two meanings: a psychological advancement in feelings of self-worth, self-confidence, and self-actualization; to gain official or legal power
Entitlements	The support of family or clan members, rights enshrined in national constitutions and international treaties, technical assistance from extension workers, and, in industrialized countries, social security and unemployment insurance
Gender	Refers to both sexes, despite weighting of only women's issues
Human capital	Skills, knowledge, capacity, and adaptive strategies
Institution	Has two meanings: an organization, and rules in use. The latter refers to working rules, procedures, and norms expressed in repeated actions and relationships between individuals and organizations*
Local	Pertaining to the village level of a particular rural or urban place or area
Local people	People who live in a particular rural or urban place or area*
Natural capital	Land, water, air, forestry/vegetation
Paradigm	A coherent and mutually supportive pattern of concepts, values, methods, and action amenable, or claiming to be amenable, to wide application*
Physical capital	Buildings, roads, machinery, crops/livestock

Poor	Has its common and wide meaning. This goes beyond its use as the adjective for poverty (see below) to include the broader sense of being deprived, in a bad condition, and lacking basic needs*
Poverty	A condition of lack of physical necessities, assets, and income. It includes, but is more than, income poverty.
Reality	People inhabit a world that is "real" to them, and they "know" with a certain degree of confidence that this world possesses such-and-such characteristics. However, in other societies what people "know" as "real" may be marginally or entirely different.
Social capital	Governance structures, decision-making power, community institutions, culture, participatory processes

---

* From Robert Chambers, *Whose Reality Counts?: Putting the Last First* (London: Intermediate Technology Publications, 1997).

Introduction

In early 1988 in south central India, more than fifty farmers committed suicide. The farmers were poor and for the most part landless tenants who had been persuaded to abandon their traditional food crop of rice in favor of what one Indian newspaper calls "the often fatal attraction of cash crops." The majority were indebted to local moneylenders at an annual interest rate of 36 percent, since no other source of credit was available to them. Instead of turning a profit, the cotton they had planted was attacked by pests and the crops failed. To make matters worse, the farmers had tried to ward off the infestation by applying three to four times the amount of pesticides required. This not only increased their indebtedness but also severely damaged the local environment and further reduced crop yields.

The above example illustrates how development interventions can go tragically awry. This example also shows that, if the right elements had been in place, such a tragedy might have been prevented. For example, credit could have been made available to the farmers at a fair interest rate, and they could have been encouraged to save. There could have been access to reliable and ecologically sound technical expertise to deal with the pest infestation. There could have been policies designed to support the farmers' livelihoods systems. Secure, productive, and sustainable livelihoods could have enabled the farmers to cope in a challenging environment. Sustainable livelihoods, therefore, may help foster resilience in people, enabling them to rebound and survive despite impending disasters.

The basic contentions of this book are implicit in its title; namely, that the poor have access to reservoirs of wealth that can be tapped and augmented through the Sustainable Livelihoods (SL) approach. This book examines the philosophies and principles that make up the

SL approach and describes, in anecdotal terms, how this approach or aspects of it have thus far been applied in various parts of the world.

The SL approach to poverty eradication, as currently practiced by UNDP, is still in its infancy. Nevertheless, many of the ideas that make up this approach, including the thinking of Paulo Freire, Robert Chambers, and others, have been well known in development circles for decades. Thus, while none of the individual components of the SL approach is new, the synergy created when key elements are combined is what makes SL so effective and distinguishes it from other development methodologies.

It is our intention to introduce readers—development professionals and nonprofessionals alike—to the principles, philosophy, and hands-on experience of the Sustainable Livelihoods approach, and also to provide a guide for implementing this approach successfully.

Adaptive Strategies
and Sustainable Livelihoods

The province of Tuléar in Southern Madagascar is a parched, waterless wasteland. In order to obtain water, people in the coastal village of Beheloka dig small pits in the sand. The water they find, however, is only slightly less brackish than the water available from their shallow wells, and only a little less likely to cause disease.

An outsider would assume that the people of Tuléar Province need access to potable water. But when the men, women, and fishermen of the village discussed their livelihoods, what they have, what they use, and how they make their living, they revealed a different priority. Counter-intuitive to the expectations of outsiders, the people did not identify water as a problem. Instead, they said that if they could catch and sell more fish, their water problem would be solved, because they could buy water from five kilometers away.

"Suppose we had given them water," says UNDP Assistant Resident Representative Lalao Ramanarivo, "then what? As outsiders, we couldn't see it at first, but water would not have strengthened their livelihoods. What they really wanted was to learn how to catch more fish, how to process the fish to make it more commercially attractive, how to market the fish more profitably. You can see the logic of their thinking. With an increase in income, not only would they be able to buy water, but they'd be able to do many other things as well. This is the basis of sustainable livelihoods."

For over half a century, efforts to promote people-centered, sustainable development in the world's poorest countries have met with, at best, mixed results. Many approaches have been tried and, in some sectors, have succeeded. For example, as a result of efforts targeted at the health and gender sectors, basic health care has improved (except where overwhelmed by the AIDS epidemic), and women's participation in development has increased. But real progress in eradicating, or even alleviating, the root causes of widespread poverty has remained elusive.

This is largely because many development experts have focused too narrowly on single issues and have failed to see the larger, multifaceted development picture. By dividing development work into "sectors" and "issues"—health, gender, food security, environment, income-generation, and so on—the cohesive, dynamic interplay or synergy of all these elements in the actual lives of real people has often been overlooked. The tendency to reduce a community into separate compartments precludes acknowledging the wholeness of the community's situation.

In 1994, however, a cross-thematic approach to poverty eradication, powered by the energies and talents of poor people, was identified. The Sustainable Livelihoods (SL) approach naturally reveals the multi-sectoral character of real life, so that development work is better able to address actual problems as they exist at the village level. SL is an integrative framework, an opportunity to promote the sort of cross-sectoral and cross-thematic approach that should be the hallmark of development work.

The SL methodology is not a program. It is an approach that builds on the fundamental building blocks of development, including income-generation, environmental management, women's empowerment, education, health care, appropriate technology, financial services, and good governance. SL seeks to set these building blocks in place in such a way that their combination and interaction create a powerful synergy, and sustainable livelihoods are the result. The philosophy is built on ideas such as *adaptive strategies, participation and empowerment, science and technology, financial services,* and *governance and policy.*

Adaptive strategies

The Sustainable Livelihoods approach is different from other approaches that examine poverty by conducting a community needs assessment. Focusing on poverty and needs consistently distracts development experts from what SL advocates believe must be the fundamental building blocks of any development initiative: the actual livelihood systems of the poor and the adaptive strategies they employ to maintain these livelihoods in the face of severe environmental, economic, and political pressures. Therefore, the SL approach begins with an analysis of the "wealth" of the poor. This wealth may reveal itself through various kinds of assets, the knowledge, skills, resourcefulness, and adaptive strategies that have enabled the poor to survive over the years, often against terrible odds. Adaptive strategies—the changes and adjustments people make in their livelihood systems in order to cope under difficult circumstances—serve as the entry point of the SL approach.

The strategies that enable the poor all over the world to overcome crises and survive hardships are often simple decisions, or coping mechanisms, that enable them to respond to an emergency. When these temporary changes continue to be applied over time and become part of everyday life, the SL methodology calls them adaptive strategies. For example, farmers in Nyamawende, Malawi, have adjusted to steadily decreasing rainfall by planting drought-resistant crops such as sweet potatoes and soybeans. Agro-pastoralists in Ethiopia mix cattle, sheep, goats, and camels in herds in order to adapt to changing conditions of climate, water and vegetation. In southern Zimbabwe, herders in the village of Mlambaphele have kept their cattle alive for decades in severe drought conditions by moving them for six months each year to a grazing area along the banks of a river.

These adaptive strategies and the livelihoods they support are sustainable: They are economically efficient, they do not consume resources that will be needed for the future, and they do not infringe on or disrupt the options of others to make their own livelihood. However, as with most adaptive strategies, there is room for improvement. A basic tenet of the SL approach is that most adaptive strategies can be made more productive, and more sustainable, with the application of a little contemporary knowledge, technology, financial services, or improvements in government policies. SL is the means by which the external can be married to the local, and outsiders can make sustainable contributions to people's livelihoods.

Activities, assets, and entitlements

A key feature of the SL approach is the recognition that the root of all human development and economic growth is livelihoods—not jobs per se, but the wide, infinitely diverse range of activities people engage in to make their living. These activities are made up of more than jobs (or variations thereof) or economic activities. In addition to activities, livelihoods consist of assets. Assets can be identified as four different types of capital: human capital (such as knowledge, skills, creativity, adaptive strategies); physical capital (such as buildings, roads, machinery, crops/livestock); natural capital (such as land/soil, air, water, forestry/vegetation); and social capital (such as governance structures, decision-making power, community groups, and culture). Livelihoods also depend on entitlements, such as the support of family or clan members that can be called upon in an emergency. In industrialized countries, where the concept of Sustainable Livelihoods also applies, such entitlements include social security, unemployment insurance, and other government-funded "safety nets."

Everyone's livelihood, however meager, is made up of these three components—activities, assets, and entitlements—together with the short-term coping mechanisms and long-term adaptive strategies that the person employs in times of crisis so that in adjusting to hardship, loss, and change, he or she can maintain a livelihood.

Understanding the current livelihood activities, assets, and entitlements of a community or individual naturally provides the best guide to understanding how their livelihoods can be made more productive and more sustainable. Sometimes an economic activity needs support, as in the case of the fishermen in Madagascar. Sometimes assets can be made more productive. Sometimes entitlements in the form of government support can be expanded, such as technical assistance from extension workers. In all these cases, helping to enhance existing livelihoods is the key to igniting a self-propelled engine of sustainable, human-centered development.

To accomplish this, the SL approach requires changes in thinking at every level, from development policy-makers to villagers. These changes in thinking are nothing less than paradigm shifts or the overturning of long-held conceptions of what is real and true. For example, in the past, traditional labor market/job analysis has been applied in an attempt to provide jobs for poor people. This has always failed, and it will continue to fail, because it does not grapple with the ways poor people actually make their living. The poor almost never *have* jobs, but they are always *doing* jobs. They are largely self-employed, with an entire range of activities, assets, and entitlement that allow them to survive.

Even in industrialized countries, where the concept of jobs took root during the industrial revolution, an exclusive focus on jobs is no longer appropriate. Politicians in the West claim to have created millions of jobs, but in countries such as the United States, earnings from such jobs are often inadequate to feed or house a family. And in developing countries, even high-status jobs frequently fail to provide livelihoods. For example, an Assistant Permanent Secretary in an African government was selling tomatoes in his office and sending his children to sell candies and cigarettes in the streets to supplement his income. This man had a job, almost a permanent job, yet he was unable to derive an adequate livelihood from it.

The story of this official also illustrates the blurred distinction that exists today between the "formal" and "informal" sectors. There could be nothing more formal than the man's government job, yet his livelihood depends on a number of activities, such as home-based agriculture and street vending, that are typical of the informal sector. More and more people, especially in developing countries, do not distinguish between the formal and informal sectors as they struggle to make ends meet.

Sustainability

What makes livelihoods—in the formal or informal sector—sustainable? What does sustainability really mean? Narrowly viewed, sustainability is often used in reference to environmental or cross-generational sustainability. In other words, it may be defined as the management and use of natural resources to ensure that these resources will remain intact for future generations. Broadly speaking, sustainability is a key indicator of success or failure in development projects. "The development field," says Thierry Lemaresquier, director of UNDP's Social Development and Poverty Elimination Division, "is littered with casualties of projects that did well for a period of time but were not sufficiently anchored. Projects that are based on empowerment and improvement in the livelihoods of the poor stand a much better chance of surviving once the initial funding and effort has run out of gas."

The SL approach is not a fixed template or formula. Instead, it is an intellectual reminder of the multi-dimensionality of community life, and of the fact that all the bases of this multi-dimensionality must be covered. Therein lies the promise of sustainability. The SL approach helps ensure sustainability in its broadest sense because it aims to understand livelihood systems and to examine such areas as natural resource endowment and the relationship of communities to policy and local governance. This raises comprehension among development practitioners about the conditions that have to be met if their efforts are to be sustained over time.

The SL approach is designed to promote four essential characteristics: economic efficiency, social equity, ecological integrity, and resilience.

Economic efficiency

To be sustainable, a livelihood system must be economically efficient, rather than wasteful, in its use of resources. For example, the organic mini-farm (1,200 square meters) of Stoitcho Ainarov and his wife in the Bulgarian village of Vinogradetz is typical of the extraordinarily productive and efficient household farms that are proliferating in that country. The Ainarovs would starve on his pension of about US$35 per month, but instead they enjoy an abundant variety of foods grown organically on their own farm. In addition to poultry, milk, wood, mutton, and goat's milk, the farm-cum-orchard produces an assortment of nuts, fruits, vegetables, wine, and animal fodder. The house, stables, and corrals take up only 200 square meters of their land. The remaining 1,000 square meters are cultivated intensively, most of it twice a year. Careful crop rotation prevents diseases and maintains soil productivity. Many resources are used more than once. Grass and alfalfa, for example, provide food for the animals, which, in turn, provide manure, or natural fertilizer, for the farm. Firewood purchased for heating and cooking is converted to ash that is also used to enrich the soil. All the fertilizer used is therefore organic, contributed either by animals as manure or in the form of ash and agricultural wastes.

Comparing this fully organic model of economically (not to mention ecologically) efficient agriculture with that practiced in the United States shows that one calorie of food is produced in the United States for every ten calories of external inputs spent (in the form of electric power, fuels, lubricants, machinery, transportation, pesticides, and herbicides), while in Bulgaria, ten calories are produced for every one calorie of external inputs.

Social equity

To be sustainable, livelihoods must adhere to the precepts of social equity; that is, the way one household or community makes its livelihood must not disrupt options for others to make theirs. Whenever possible, one form of livelihood should enhance other livelihoods, as in relationships of trade, exchange, and services. Such social equity and community loyalty are also exemplified by the Ainarovs, who prefer to sell their grapes to the village cooperative for BGL 200 per kilogram rather than to merchants from the city for BGL 300. "I have to be fair to my co-op," says Ainarov, reflecting his society's belief that being a part of a trust network is important.

There are, however, countless exploitative relationships throughout the world, where the livelihoods of one group—from moneylenders and middlemen to landowners, industrialists, and other employers—are often based on practices that restrict, hamper, or threaten the livelihoods of others. Take the Zamindars in Bangladesh, a group serving as feudal landlords paying the government a fixed revenue. Their livelihoods have been maintained by closing the options of others. However, work conducted by Bengali NGOs such as the Grameen Bank, the Bangladesh Rural Advancement Committee (BRAC), and Proshika are empowering the poor. For every difficult situation in which one group closes the options for others, more and more innovative solutions are being found.

Ecological integrity

To be sustainable, livelihood systems must obey the laws of ecological integrity, preserving or restoring resources for use by future generations. The way people make their livelihoods must not destroy the resource base. Livelihoods do consume resources, but they must live off the interest and not exhaust the capital. The alarming rate of forest destruction for fuel wood throughout the world is a tragic example of how the poor are being forced to live off the capital of one of earth's most precious resources.

The Malawian villages of Nyamawende and Gandali identified the availability of clean drinking water as one of their priorities for action. The villagers understood that it was essential for women to boil drinking water to prevent diarrhea and other diseases, particularly among children. But the additional fuel wood needed to boil the water was unavailable in Gandali, which is located in an almost totally deforested area. In Nyamawende, too, wood for fuel is so scarce and the surrounding forests are dwindling so fast that the people have decided to launch an intensive reforestation effort and carefully to restrict the cutting of fuel wood around their village. The SL initiative identified a simple, low-tech machine (produced by a US-based NGO called Stanlinks) that turns leaves, brush, and other agricultural waste into energy-efficient, clean-burning briquettes. Groups of women in neighboring villages were using this machine to produce briquettes that they sold on the local market at a price lower than that of fuel wood. When the women of Gandali and Nyamawende discovered that three briquettes could cook a traditional Malawian meal of *nsima* (corn porridge) or boil water for six minutes to make it safe for drinking, they wanted to acquire the machine and make briquettes for themselves. In a small country like Malawi, where 5.5 million cubic meters of fuel wood are consumed per year, ecologically efficient technologies like this one are urgently needed to establish environmental sustainability.

Resilience

Finally, to be sustainable, livelihood systems must be resilient. They must be able to cope with, and recover from, shocks and stresses. They must be flexible enough, and the people involved in them resilient and resourceful enough, to employ effective mechanisms for surviving in times of crisis. When these coping mechanisms prove effective enough to be employed over an extended period of time, as previously mentioned, they become what the SL paradigm calls adaptive strategies.

Sustainable Livelihoods and gender

The roles of men and women are imbued with different meanings in different societies, and these meanings are reinforced by traditions that socialize people around their respective gender roles. Some ideas must be affirmed continuously; one of these is the fact that men and women experience life differently. Therefore, it is important to solicit information about assets and adaptive strategies from men *and* women.

The SL paradigm insists that it is essential to acknowledge openly and take into account the distinctive roles of women and the special obstacles they face, as well as the different social situations of women and men and the frequently unequal sharing of resources within each household. For example, an analysis of adaptive strategies conducted on a community basis must take into account the fact that women's adaptive strategies within the household may be different from men's. SL can serve as the vehicle to recognize each gender's fundamental sources of strength and sustenance.

Gender-specific research is expanding appreciation of all human beings by looking at what makes each sex unique. For example, separating men and women's groups to discuss their perceptions of their village's problems is important. Men and women may have collective strategies. When they do, the barriers and obstacles that women experience in their lives—and in their economic activities—will have an overall depressing impact on these household strategies. To assess what sustainable household strategies might be, facilitators need to be trained to encourage household members to discuss the issue of gender roles and factor it into their strategies.

Promoting Sustainable Livelihoods

It is essential to remember what Sustainable Livelihoods is *not*. Sustainable Livelihoods is not merely basic needs or subsistence living. Meeting basic needs is only the first step. SL is a reminder of the complexity of development, but also of the uniqueness of situations at the people's level. It can help establish a development agenda that is focused on the key issues of sustainability, of legitimacy—turning over development to the democratic process—and of empowerment. SL is a combination of a number of approaches, using elements of each. However, none of these approaches by itself can produce the same effect, the same level of genuine participatory empowerment, that the SL approach can achieve.

For example, integrated rural development is largely a donor-driven exercise. Donors who are doing different projects try to bring these projects together in an integrated framework, an inherently "top-down" approach in which villagers have little or no voice. This system is largely based on consultation rather than participation, and its objectives are usually donor objectives, not the objectives of the people. First the project is designed, and *then* the people are consulted and expected to participate. This does not work. With the SL approach, outsiders participate in local people's projects. "Promoting sustainable livelihoods involves determining what people already know," says B. T. Costantinos, team leader of UNDP's SL program in Malawi. "How do they adapt over time? What kinds of changes have taken place within their livelihood systems to enable them to adapt to new environments? And, most important, how can they make these livelihoods more sustainable?" Support for existing livelihoods that ensures sustainability and seeks to increase productivity is the essence of the SL approach. After determining what the community already does well, the SL approach begins the process of augmenting these adaptive strategies and assets. The interactive, participatory components include:

- Understanding adaptive strategies;
- Analyzing current policies and governance issues that impinge on people's livelihood strategies;
- Identifying appropriate technology that can improve productivity;
- Identifying social and economic mechanisms that can help existing livelihoods strategies by improving, producing, or creating new opportunities;
- Developing SL indicators to monitor the progress of different programs.

It is imperative to remember that these components are not linear or sequential. They should be undertaken simultaneously and interactively so that the synergy that produces sustainable livelihoods can take place. For the purposes of clarity, however, the components have been separated into chapters. This is not intended to reduce the approach into its parts but to make the SL process clear to the reader.

2

Participation and Empowerment

The real purpose of development is to achieve empowerment within the individual.

—*Peter Jere*
SL facilitator, Malawi

Traditionally, development has been defined in terms of infrastructure. But development should focus on people, their attitudes and practices, and on the process of change in these attitudes and practices. Development that is sustainable changes people's attitudes and practices so that they can choose to take responsibility for, or reject, aspects of their situation. In other words, it empowers them. After individuals are empowered, they take responsibility for their own development, including looking after the infrastructural matters that complement the changes that have taken place within them. Phosiso Sola is a Zimbabwean environmental botanist who has been applying the SL approach for some time. "The most effective aspect of this approach is the idea of empowerment," she says. "It destroys any chances of initiating the donor-dependency syndrome. People really feel they are part of the system, not 'parcels' in the system. It does work. When we told [the people], 'We would like to look at what you have and what works here,' they really wanted to show off. 'After all,' they said, 'the answers are within us. They are not from outside.'"

Brazilian educator Paulo Freire introduced the concept of participatory development in 1970. In *Pedagogy of the Oppressed*, Freire describes what he calls "training for transformation," a method for teaching illiterate adults how to think critically about themselves, their circumstances, and the world around them. The concept of participatory development was a reaction to the development policies of the 1970s that fostered relationships of economic dependency on governments and donors. The communities targeted by these "top-down" development policies were not acknowledged as legitimate stakeholders in their own development process. Realizing the short-coming of this paradigm led to the popularization of participatory development, in which facilitators focus on a community's assets, strategies, and strengths rather than its needs. As a result, a sense of equality, rather than inferiority, develops between villagers and development workers. More recently, such ideas have been carried forward and expanded by development thinkers such as Robert Chambers and David Korten.

From its inception, the SL approach set out to shatter stereotypes about "superior" outsiders as compared to "ignorant" villagers. As discussed in chapter 1, adaptive strategies are regarded as local knowledge. Therefore, facilitators must first develop an understanding of the community's knowledge, then bring in their technical know-how and contemporary knowledge to supplement what the community already knows.

The words *people's participation* have become a mantra in development discourse. But genuine commitment to real participation is another matter entirely. "People may talk the right talk," says Kristine Jones, SL advisor to the National Economic Council of Malawi, "but very often what development workers are doing in the field is not transformative and it's not participatory and it doesn't really listen to the people." For this reason, facilitators need careful training. They must be made aware of the need to overcome their preconceptions so that they can understand the wealth of the poor.

Training for facilitators

In many developing countries, the legacy of colonialism combined with cultural and social traditions has left behind a rigid social hierarchy. Members of the educated elite, even if they are engaged in "development" work, carefully maintain a personal distance and sense of superiority in all their interactions with the poor. This phenomenon can be a serious obstacle to the empowerment of the poor. Development workers need assiduous attitudinal training if they are to help villagers start the process of community consciousness-raising needed to reshape their expectations of development workers and of themselves.

Most people involved with SL agree that careful training and "sensitizing" are crucial to success. Long-held preconceptions and prejudices can persist, even among people with experience in so-called participatory development. To *listen* to poor people is a new reality, a reversal of the more familiar "top-down" interventions. "It's not only the villagers who need transformation," says Peter Jere, SL facilitator in Malawi, "it's the facilitators themselves." A three- to four-week training session that focuses on concepts and belief paradigms is the most effective training, although not long enough to bring about the deep-rooted transformation of attitudes and practices that sustainable development requires. Therefore, facilitators should continue to be self-critical during the entire process of working with a community. "Facilitators," says Jere, "have to reflect on their performance, and probably on their attitude, *every* day. Otherwise they may end up lecturing or simply feeding people information."

If you reach a point where your own attitude is actually transformed, you perceive whatever the people do more positively, and you can see it as an opportunity to maybe adjust yourself. You do not blame them for things. Instead, you learn why they are doing whatever it is. If they do not come to a meeting, you do not get frustrated. You understand there is a reason why they did not come, and you have to find out what it is. You do not just say, "Oh, these people are lazy, they do not want to come to discuss with us."

—Peter Jere, SL facilitator, Malawi

Training for villagers

Even more than economic conditions, attitudes and ingrained patterns of thinking determine the resourcefulness and resilience of a community. In many cultures throughout the developing world, the ravages of history have stifled individual initiative, confidence, and self-reliance. According to B. T. Costantinos, team leader of UNDP's SL program in Malawi, "Malawians today are saddled with a background of century-old colonialism during which they were told they were slaves, that they were not human beings, and thirty years of dictatorship that has disempowered them to the point where they think of themselves as second-class citizens. So there is an element of fatalism, of discouragement, of disempowerment among these people." Can three weeks of consciousness-raising through parables, discussions, and role-plays begin to chip away at the demoralizing effects of decades of colonialism and centralized authoritarianism, broken promises, and paternalistic policies? It can.

Community consciousness-raising increases a community's awareness of its behaviors and experiences. The purpose is to help villagers look at themselves in order to discover how they have internalized their social and cultural reality and how they can explore new options. Facilitated by development workers, this process usually occurs in discussion groups in which community members come together on a regular basis to share their personal experiences with other community members in order to gain an understanding of their own society. Together, group members explore the socialization common to their particular society and perhaps uncover common themes and messages. Profound interconnections occur when the community experiences awareness and insight into the value of its own adaptive strategies and community "knowledge." After participating in such groups, people tend to become stronger, more self-confident, proud of a newfound identity, and empowered.

Participatory research

There are several different styles and methods of participatory research. For example, Participatory Rural Appraisal (PRA) is considered to be an eclectic style of information gathering. Practitioners become respectful listeners seeking to learn about local knowledge and promote community empowerment. Researchers who become listeners and learners can help a community identify its adaptive strategies.

PAPSL methodology

The SL research approach involves inviting people's participation and creating an enabling environment that fosters transformation of people's understanding of what they have power to do. It gives a voice to people where they had none before.

Participatory Assessment and Planning for Sustainable Livelihoods (PAPSL) is a fusion of three development methodologies:

- Training for Transformation, which seeks to "awaken" and "empower" the poor to take charge of their own development;

- Participatory Rural Appraisal (PRA), a system of research and information gathering that involves local people in a detailed study of their community and livelihood systems; and
- a planning methodology designed to produce strategies for action.

The PAPSL guidebook is the first development handbook that combines these three approaches into a single process. It is an effective tool that builds on the various styles of participatory research and guides facilitators as they seek to empower villagers.

The PAPSL methodology proposes six steps of project execution. In order for this kind of empowerment and transformation in thinking to take place, the groundwork must be laid in advance. The first step of the PAPSL process consists in identifying and conceptualizing projects and outlining the responsibilities of sponsoring international agencies to coordinate them. The second step addresses the principles needed to select countries in which to conduct participatory research, including preliminary groundwork to identify the sites and communities for fieldwork. Step three consists of in-country preparations. Facilitators must collect formal permissions and clearances as they consider how to translate the project concepts in a manner that will be understood by local people. It is also important to be sure the people understand the active role they will be called upon to play and the fact that they should not expect infusions of money or other "hand-outs" to result from the process.

The section on climate-setting in the PAPSL guide describes a number of steps designed to develop open relationships of mutual trust with community members. These include:

- An informal walk around the community with a group of community members.
- "Icebreakers" or warm-up exercises to help make participants feel relaxed. Such exercises may seem trivial or childish to those unused to seeing them in a development context, but similar methods designed to encourage teamwork and fruitful interaction are being found increasingly effective in the business world.
- An introduction to the PAPSL team, including personal introductions by all team members and participants; an explanation of the purpose of the PAPSL process; discussion of the length of stay of the team; discussion of timing, in which the community

decides when it would like to work with the team on a daily basis; segmentation of interaction groups for future meetings (for example, farmers, young women, older women, young men, older men, community organizations and youth).

- A discussion of expectations to clear up any misconceptions and to explain which expectations can be met.

- A review of participatory fieldwork methods and techniques, such as discussions, complete with illustrative diagrams of issues such as development, liberation, and multi-track communications. Participants are helped to view themselves in the context of their community, their country, and their environment, and to understand the potential for fruitful communication to take place between all levels of society and the state.

- A policy analysis that examines the policies that impinge on local livelihood realities. Community members discuss whether their problems result from the failure of the government or the community. If it is a community problem, how can they take action?

- A final step outlines the output and follow-up.

Central to the PAPSL exercise is a detailed assessment and analysis of livelihoods systems, including the gathering of precise information on the physical features of the community, its resources, assets, infrastructure, and activities. The process also includes selecting volunteers for a community-based monitoring group that meets with the team of facilitators every two days to give feedback about community reactions to the program and to discuss how interactions with the community could be improved. In addition, these volunteers help facilitators with an ongoing "listening survey," a method of identifying which issues are most crucial to the community by systematic listening at all discussions. Issues identified by the listening survey are then classified through group discussions according to whether each issue poses a need, an opportunity, a problem, or a solution. A chart containing these headings is maintained and added to throughout the entire PAPSL process. Such exercises in analytical thinking encourage problem solving and foster within community members a sense of confidence that they can identify ways to improve their own lives.

As a result of all these interactions, people get the message that they are capable of solving their own problems. The community is empowered to understand its situation and its problems. In an organic, informal way, all these discussions lead naturally to the compiling of Action Plans. "In the village of Nyamawende," says Peter Jere, "the process of analyzing and preparing Action Plans was ongoing. There was no specific time when we stopped doing assessments and started action-planning. When issues came up, we analyzed them, then we moved right on to action-planning, with the people suggesting the solutions." The SL approach helps people analyze their problems and arrive at the root causes; based on an understanding of these root causes, they come up with solutions.

Women are central to development

Aside from the moral imperative, there is a highly practical reason for ensuring that women participate in the SL process. Women are usually the chief engine of development in a community. Indeed, history makes it evident that women are responsible for the majority of development activities in the village. They are usually the group that will later implement the Action Plans, because they are already active as the breadwinners, even in the male-headed households.

"Another important reason for including women in the PAPSL process," says Jere, "is that the participatory method was developed to try to capture the voice of the poor, the voice of those who own poverty in the communities. This group largely consists of women. So it is very important that facilitators discuss issues with the people who own poverty, the people who are sidelined."

"Even though women are the principal workers, they are largely passive in the development process. Usually they are involved only in a mechanical way, for the use of their energy to carry water, to mold bricks, and so on, but are not involved in decision-making. Yet they are a resource, and it is necessary to maximize their potential."

Women are the ones who feel responsible, while men spend most of their income on irrelevant activities. I feel that the women's involvement was very helpful because they are the key players.
—Peter Jere, SL facilitator, Malawi

Case study

The Sustainable Livelihoods approach was first applied as a methodology in August 1997 in a comprehensive, country-wide government program aimed to help villagers articulate and elaborate their own plans for the development of their communities. As part of a UNDP-supported government program designed to promote food security by strengthening the livelihood systems of the poor, SL was introduced in five villages in Mchinji District in western Malawi. It was expected to be operating in six or seven of Malawi's twenty-five districts by the end of 1998.

In the village of Nyamawende, the community had to be prepared carefully before the six Malawian facilitators applied the PAPSL methodology. This included going through the District Development Committee. The newly democratic political climate in Malawi provided an ideal context for explaining the purpose of the assessment process. The facilitators explained that the program was trying to complement the democratic process by involving the community in developing its own Action Plans. It is essential clearly and completely to inform the authorities in a community of the purpose of the assessment process, and to explain how it differs from other visits by development workers that may have taken place in the past.

Nyamawende consists of a string of small, mud-brick huts with thatch roofs that stretches between two denuded hills along the main road to Zambia in western Malawi. Nyamawende faces problems that are typical

Figure 2-1 Map of Malawi

of thousands of villages all over the developing world. Malnutrition in children is common. Clean water is scarce. Wood for fuel is hard to come by, and deforestation is accelerating. The soil is nearly exhausted. More than one-third of the men and two-thirds of the women are illiterate. Of the community's 300 families, only seven children attend secondary school. Even so, most of the villagers do not perceive themselves as poor. The people of Nyamawende identified 124 of the village's 223 households as "better off." These families have at least six acres of land; their brick or mud houses are thatched with grass; they have at least three head of cattle and one goat, one granary of maize, one ox cart, and one bicycle. Of the remaining families, 94 were considered "poor" (no bicycle, no livestock, no food stores), and five were labeled "very poor." None was considered "very rich."

The people of Nyamawende began working on their problems by taking the first step in the SL methodology—a three-week assessment and planning process to identify the assets, entitlements, activities, and knowledge base of their community. Participatory in nature, the three-week assessment incorporates community members into discussion groups. The high level of participation in Nyamawende was attributed to the careful preparation and "climate setting" that was done before the process began. Such climate-setting steps may seem time-consuming, but they were crucial to the success of the three-week exercise in Nyamawende. "We raised awareness about our objectives, goals, and the approach we were going to take," says Peter Jere. "And we involved the community in structuring the way we were going to go about the discussions."

Groups convened regularly to share personal experiences with other community members, to gain an understanding of their own society, and to explore the socialization common to their particular community. SL facilitators guided the process to emphasize the strengths and adaptive strategies of the community's livelihoods. "Often we did not even convene a meeting," says Jere. "The six of us on the team split up and worked individually or in twos. We just chatted with women at the bore hole, with men at a beer party, with a family over a meal of *nsima*. You just find yourself there and you start talking. And if you have convened a group discussion, afterward when you disperse you can still interact with the people informally, and those informal interactions are usually more revealing than the meeting itself. They tell you the real situation in the community." This informality carried through to every aspect of the assessment process, Jere says.

Key to building trust was that the facilitators settled down to live in the village for the full three weeks of the assessment process, even remaining on weekends to spend additional time with the villagers. "We did not consider whether it was Saturday or Sunday," says Jere. "We just lived among the people for the whole three weeks. On Sunday we went to their church, and we went with them to the installation ceremony of a chief in a neighboring village. They were so impressed by these small things that they opened up to us. On that day, all over the community, women started bringing in drums and dancing. We had already been there a week, but this was their way of really welcoming us and making us feel at home."

The PAPSL process conducted in Nyamawende was a free-wheeling, eclectic combination of informal interviews, group discussions, casual chats under a tree, and strolls through the village. It also included role-plays, stories or parables, and analytical devices such as the "Problem Tree," which diagrams the components of a problem from its root causes to its branching effects, and stimulates people to analyze the circumstances in which they live.

Coming together to analyze a problem and devise a solution had not been part of the local culture. But exercises such as the Problem Tree opened new possibilities to the people. They began to see that they could do something about their problems. "When you do the Problem Tree, you ask the question: Why?" says Peter Kulemeka, UNDP's Assistant Resident Representative and SL program manager in Malawi. "Then you look at the root causes and you begin to see why a certain thing is happening. This makes people realize, 'Oh, we can do something about this. We don't have to depend on outsiders all the time.'" In Nyamawende, the Problem Tree methodology

---

One role-play was designed to illustrate the problem of having too many children to provide for adequately. One of the village women mobilized about twelve children aged between four and five. After pretending to cook, two of the children came and collected the food on two plates and went to sit with the other children. They all scrambled over the food. When they had finished all the food, the others were there crying, saying, "We want more to eat." People started reacting even before the play was over because they recognized that the situation existed in their community. It made a big impression on them. It is a very effective technique.

—Peter Jere, SL facilitator, Malawi

helped villagers initiate a community police force to guard against thieves and cattle-rustlers.

As a result of a recent devaluation of the local currency, imported chemical fertilizers had become prohibitively expensive for small-scale farmers. Initially, people blamed the government, claiming that their community was not being adequately assisted. However, since this problem resulted from market forces, technical issues such as the relationship between currency devaluation and the local economy were discussed with community members. The villagers then agreed that they were finding the situation difficult to understand because they had little control over the conditions that caused it. When they agreed that the high fertilizer prices were out of their control, they began looking for alternatives. The community then arrived at the idea of producing compost manure, which is a much better solution and much more sustainable.

In order to ensure that a good cross-section of the population (men, women, young, old) was represented in the discussions and other activities, a very informal system of separating and mixing the various groups was implemented. Indeed, the very process of meeting in this way gave members of the community an opportunity to share information with one another as they never had before. For example, malnutrition was clearly a problem in the community, especially among young children. But with the exception of a few women, 90 percent of the people did not know their diet was unbalanced and lacked essential nutrients that could be provided by a wider variety of food crops. During group discussions about nutrition, the few women who had knowledge of nutrition were able to share their knowledge for the first time. This in turn lead to the formulation of several of the community's Action Plans relating to improving nutrition.

In general, the participation of women in Nyamawende was unusually high. This was due to the fact that the village is on a main road and near the district headquarters at Mchinji; the women were used to strangers and were far less shy than women in more isolated communities, who almost never spoke up during PAPSL discussions. "In this community it was totally different," says Jere. "Women actually talked more than men, to the point where they would even call the men to speak. The women would say, 'You are not saying anything, can you also speak?'"

Clearly, the participation of women in Nyamawende helped to bring out important issues, such as the need for clean drinking water and fuel wood, which did not come up in discussions with men alone. At first men did not consider the chronic scarcity of water and fuel to be problems, because the responsibility for providing both these commodities rests solely with the women.

A role-play was used to raise the issue of excessive beer drinking, which was clearly a problem in the community. At first the villagers denied that this was a problem, and the men especially refused to discuss it further. Instead, the problem of an unbalanced diet was discussed. In analyzing the root causes of this problem using the Problem Tree, villagers concluded that the reason some children were not adequately fed was that excessive beer drinking made some men neglect their responsibilities to their families. A role-play was conducted in which a couple is on its way to work on their farm, but instead they stop off at a beer party and never arrive at the farm to work at all. Many people watching this role-play laughed with a sense of recognition and admitted that this was a problem they knew only too well. These discussions in turn led to an analysis of the problem. As a result, tucked away in the pages of several of Nyamawende's Action Plans are initiatives designed to discourage excessive beer drinking, such as participating in Family Life Education sessions, promoting recreational activities such as sports, drama, and dance, and organizing youth clubs.

Some women in Nyamawende already served as role models for the community. "We had a woman who is a very, very successful farmer," Peter Jere says, "probably the most successful in the village. She has the largest grain store in the village. A real role model. We also had a traditional medicine person who was a woman, the only one in the village." These women were called on several times to serve as resource persons to help other villagers, and one woman was asked to be the village literacy teacher. "We asked these women to talk about their experiences and how they managed to get to that point. We actually utilized them because we felt their voices would bear more fruit than ours."

In Nyamawende, when participants began diagramming the discussions and taking ownership of various responsibilities, they eventually produced a list of eleven Action Plans outlining pressing economic, environmental, and social problems.

The list of Nyamawende's Action Plans reads like a comprehensive program for integrated development, covering virtually all of the sectors and issues that donors usually address in isolation from one another (health, gender, agriculture, environment, nutrition, income-generation, education, child development, family planning):

- Improving nutrition with a more balanced diet by learning how to process and prepare nutritious foods such as soybeans; by planting additional drought-resistant crops such as millet and sorghum; and by holding nutrition classes for mothers
- Increasing food production by using compost manure instead of prohibitively expensive, environmentally harmful chemical fertilizers
- Restoring the degraded environment by controlling the cutting of trees, starting a woodlot, and reforesting denuded hillsides with seed provided by the forestry department
- Protecting crops and livestock from animals and thieves by tethering goats, penning pigs, and patrolling grazing areas against cattle-rustlers
- Providing safe drinking water by boiling and filtering water and adding chlorine, drilling bore holes, digging trenches, and installing taps
- Increasing adult literacy by training literate villagers as literacy teachers and setting up literacy classes for men and women
- Preparing young children to learn by training four nursery-school teachers and building two nursery schools
- Increasing incomes by starting businesses such as poultry-raising and providing training in various skills, e.g., carpentry, brick-laying, pottery, bicycle repair, tinsmithing, blacksmithing, painting, art, and tailoring
- Promoting commerce by repairing and widening five dirt roads that connect the village to other communities
- Reducing closely spaced births by encouraging the use of family planning and setting up a committee to distribute family planning methods
- Lightening women's work loads by raising awareness of the effects of overburdening women and by discouraging men from excessive beer-drinking

Most of these Action Plans fall within the outline of priorities that Malawi's SL program has developed. These priorities are environmental sustainability, enterprise development, technology, microfinance, and gender, as well as food security.

Peter Jere remembers the last day of the PAPSL process, when the Action Plans were presented to the community as a whole. "Everybody was called and there was a function, dancing, a small party and everybody was happy, celebrating. It was a celebration because they had managed to come up with Action Plans on their own that reflected their own ideas."

Directly or indirectly, all the Nyamawende Action Plans support Sustainable Livelihoods. They seek to increase productivity by improving health and developing people's capacities and skills, upgrading local technologies, and building on local knowledge. They seek to promote sustainability by protecting assets and resources and restoring and preserving the environment.

By April 1998 there was an already impressive level of energy and activity in the village. A group of about sixty villagers gathered every morning to spend three hours repairing and widening the roads. A woman's group had already started a bee-keeping enterprise with loans from the District Development Office before the SL process began. The women expected to pay off their loans soon so that they could take out new loans and start additional businesses, such as dress- and sweater-making. Women also met regularly at the home of the village's designated literacy teacher. Bricks were being made for new literacy classrooms at one of the nursery schools. Farmers had learned improved techniques for making compost manure and were ready to apply this compost to their fields for the next planting season. The cutting of wood for fuel was gradually replaced by the use of briquettes made by a simple machine that converts leaves, grasses, brush, and crop residues into an economical source of fuel.

To promote environmental sustainability, the people of Nyamawende devised a strong, multifaceted reforestation program among their Action Plans. They set up a committee to patrol a forested area to prevent the cutting of trees and to take offenders to the traditional village court to be reprimanded. They collected seeds of fast-growing indigenous trees from the Forestry Department to create woodlots and to plant on a bare hillside with a view to preventing erosion. And they weeded in the forest to prevent brushfires.

Another committee patrols livestock and farms to protect them from thieves. Although some of these initiatives were already in the works before the SL process began, the SL methodology has helped the people design plans in an organized way in order to make their livelihoods more productive and more sustainable and to take care of other local problems as well. "The planning process itself is designed to create self-awareness within communities," says B. T. Costantinos. "They realize that they can do something for themselves—create the necessary leadership and organizations for this work. Once you've done that with people, nothing stops them. They use every resource available. They change their world around them."

—— TIPS AND LESSONS LEARNED ——

♦ Focus on villagers' adaptive strategies with sufficient emphasis from the start of the assessment exercise, rather than beginning with an analysis of community problems and needs.

♦ In conjunction with the PAPSL guidebook, the book *Participatory Research for Sustainable Livelihoods* by J. Keith Rennie and Naresh C. Singh (see "Resources") is useful.

♦ "The best PRA [Participatory Rural Appraisal] manual is a blank page. At the bottom it says, 'Use your common sense'" (Robert Chambers, speaking on the value of handbooks and guides to effective assessment research).

♦ Make sure that all staff members in the district offices are comfortable with the idea that villagers are leading the development process, so that they do not revert to the old, "top-down" way of doing things, in which development plans are laid out by the authorities.

♦ If facilitators focus too much on needs and too little on adaptive strategies and other community assets, the villagers may expect hand-outs of one kind or another and be disappointed when none is forthcoming.

♦ Preliminary preparation work must be carried out carefully and thoroughly; otherwise people become very suspicious of the PAPSL teams and their motives for being in the community.

♦ To meet the expectations that are kindled by the PAPSL process, matching funds (to complement labor and other contributions by villagers) should be made available immediately so that carrying out the various projects that need financial support can begin without delay.

3

Science and Technology

Knowledge and creativity are unlimited resources.
— *Naresh C. Singh*

In many cases, strengthening a livelihood system is relatively simple. It often consists of an application of "contemporary knowledge:" science or technology that brings improvements in agriculture, industry, housing, infrastructure or communications, as well as providing training in more effective, more productive, more sustainable ways of making a living. However, effective community participation in the technology development is needed to ensure that outside technology and know-how does not dominate in the development process.

Sustainable technologies

The primary purpose of sustainable technologies is to create livelihoods—jobs that do not destroy the environment, that are good for both men and women, and that are local and small scale. The second purpose of sustainable technologies is to satisfy basic needs—shelter, water, energy, clothing, paper—that people do not have any other way to satisfy. Ashok Khosla, president of Development Alternatives, a large NGO based in New Delhi, points out that there is a pervasive need among both the rural and the urban poor for a whole variety of technologies. When looking at a need, such as the mushrooming demand for affordable housing for the poor in India, it is important to see other needs as well: the urgent need for millions of jobs that provide a livelihood, the need to manage resources sustainably, and the need to minimize pollution.

In a paper delivered at a workshop on Sustainable Livelihoods held in New York in November 1997, Khosla outlined the parameters of sustainable technology:

- It is relevant and ready for use by the common people, and aims directly to improve the quality of their lives.
- It derives maximum leverage from the local environment by drawing upon existing managerial and technical skills and providing the basis for extending them.
- It uses the physical potential of an area, and maintains harmony between people and nature.

These criteria are in harmony with the SL philosophy, which uses economic efficiency, social equity, ecological integrity, and resilience (the ability to withstand and recover from shocks and stresses) as its benchmarks. If technology is to strengthen livelihoods and make them sustainable, therefore, it must be "appropriate" for local needs and conditions. It must create meaningful jobs rather than eliminating them, and it must not disrupt existing livelihoods systems. It should be labor-saving rather than labor-intensive, and it must preserve, enhance and enrich the local environment rather than depleting it. According to Khosla, "a sustainable livelihood is a remunerative, satisfying and meaningful job that enables each member of the community to help nurture and re-create the resource base."

The widespread dissemination of sustainable technologies requires important changes in the way industries work, such as:

- new types of institutional structures to carry out new kinds of functions;
- decentralization of innovation, production, and marketing to respond to local needs and conditions;
- a large enough product range and territorial coverage to provide economies of scale in innovation, manufacturing, and marketing;
- development of clusters and packages of technologies to take advantage of standardized modules and components for facilitating production, marketing, spare-parts availability, and maintenance.

It is also important to overcome the little-understood obstacles to widespread dissemination of technologies for the poor. Not only is there an obvious need for a vast array of simple technologies, but there is actually no lack of designs for them as well. "Hundred of such designs are scattered in laboratories, workshops, and archives throughout the world," says Khosla. "So why has the existing technical capacity not led to supply?" The constraints are many. They include capital and operational costs; efficiency of the technology; ease of operation and ergonomic design; availability of spare parts and ease of repair and maintenance; problems of production; adaptation to local conditions; and a lack of marketing organizations, promotion, training, extension services, and management skills.

While it is important to innovate, produce, and market, the element of speed cannot be underestimated. Time must be spent optimizing existing technologies and adapting them to the users' needs. Technologies should be creative ideas that have been appropriated and optimized; this is the hallmark of what we call "liberated" technology. To be liberated a technology must be recognized as useful and able to function in any setting, without the technical, promotional, or marketing support of its parent organization.

Methodology

Introducing technology requires action on three levels. At the national level it is important to concentrate on the formulation and adoption of technology policies, such as outlining strategic goals or introducing incentives for collaboration between public and private sectors. It is also important to research and develop technologies at government scientific institutions, universities, and research centers, and to coordinate relevant stakeholders. To do this, the first step is generally to approach the host government in order to take full advantage of what it has to offer in terms of support for investment in infrastructure (roads, canals, tree planting, and so on) and social services. But the SL approach does not stop there. It aims at introducing more fundamental changes that can help communities to initiate, use, and support the transfer of modern technology, and eventually to participate in the innovation of technologies that can enhance the utilization of natural, human, physical, and social resources that are available locally.

At the intermediate level, it is important to develop institutional support. Networks can provide technology and managerial support to small businesses and microenterprises at the community level. Institutions can participate in information sharing by collecting data, and producing and disseminating comparative studies. They should also support planning at the local level by providing relevant data that can serve as a basis for sound assessment of resources and present technology levels and policies. They can also document indigenous knowledge.

At the local level, facilitators should assess the current technology level, needs, and constraints. After the assessment it is important to integrate technology issues into local Action Plans and to facilitate networking.

Case studies

Development Alternatives (DA)

Ashok Khosla of Development Alternatives (DA) points out that 15 million new jobs are needed each year in India alone. To generate these, there is a need to establish sustainable enterprises—small, local businesses—in very large numbers. To promote the proliferation of small, local businesses, DA established a leasing and finance wing that works closely with the India Micro Enterprise Development Fund to establish financing systems to enable small entrepreneurs to set up local businesses based on technologies the organization has developed.

DA has found some two hundred local entrepreneurs in various parts of India and has set them up as franchises in the tile-making business. These "bosses" receive business support from DA but no subsidies or financial aid in purchasing a machine. "My entrepreneurs have got a little money, they can go to the bank, they can borrow, and they can run a business," says Khosla. "Without them, how am I going to create ten stable jobs in the village?"

DA's staff of more than five hundred, scattered throughout every state in India, includes anthropologists and sociologists who make frequent field trips to investigate potential products for development. "They come back and tell us, 'You know, there would be a terrific market if you could develop a machine to make rope. We found a community that has a certain kind of fiber and biomass which could make excellent rope, but they do not have the tools and the implements to do it.'"

One such innovation, a machine that makes a new kind of roofing tile out of stone dust, sand, and a little cement, went through seven years of detailed market research and design before becoming one of DA's most successful technologies for job creation. "The tiles are easy to construct," says Khosla. "The stone dust comes from quarries and is a pollutant, so people pay you to take it away. The tiles are as cheap as thatch, and they last about ten times as long." He explains that one tile-making machine costs about $3,500 as a capital investment and produces about 200 tiles a day, creating about ten jobs for workers who make the tiles and install them on roofs.

The number of businesses making tiles tends to double in little over a year, and the organization launched a campaign to bring the number of tile-making franchises up to one thousand by the middle of the year 2000—providing ten thousand sustainable livelihoods in about four years from one technology alone. Other people have started producing the tile-making machines as well, yet for now DA continues to manufacture them. "If we found that roofing tile machines are being made cheaper and better by other people, we would get out," says Khosla. "But it's not so easy. A lot of people make hamburgers, but McDonalds is still in the business because it provides additional services, training, know-how, quality control, standardization, all kinds of innovations. We're in that business too." Khosla explains that DA not only provides technical support, help with obtaining financing from banks, and help with preparing feasibility reports, but it also buys back half of a franchise's tiles the first year to provide market support. In addition, DA trains its entrepreneurs in marketing, promotion, and advertising. "And we have RATF, our Rapid Action Task Force," Khosla says. "They go around the countryside and they guarantee that within twenty-four hours of any breakdown, your machines will be up and working again if you have a franchise agreement with us. You can't have a business idle for five days if it's going to pay salaries to ten people."

DA's most widely distributed product is a simple, fuel-efficient cooking stove that burns twigs, biomass, briquettes, or charcoal and consumes about 50 percent less fuel than traditional stoves. It costs about $3 to make and just a little more to buy. "We started selling the stoves through franchises, and we got to a stage where they were being pirated by people—copied and sold—because they were very simple and cheap to make," says Khosla. "So we encouraged that. We do not believe in intellectual copyrights, and why should we worry about other people making them, since that's the only way to get them out in huge numbers? All we said was, 'If you are going to copy them, copy them right.'" DA started handing out blueprints for the stoves and providing training to anyone who wanted to make them. "They are out there in very large numbers, and of course they have been further modified. Appropriate technology in my opinion is technology that is *appropriated* by the people. They get a sense of ownership; they feel it is theirs. They can modify it, they can change it, they can deal with it intelligently." In fact, the stoves are turning up far from India, and in many cases the modifications made are negligible.

In the area of energy production, DA's power unit works in partnership with local communities to establish small electrical utilities that rely exclusively on local, renewable energy sources and that use local personnel and distribution systems. The unit supplies power to domestic, commercial and small industrial users at competitive prices.

Of course, the question inevitably arises: Who pays for all the years of exhaustive research required to produce the perfect cooking stove or the perfect tile-making machine? DA is strictly nonprofit, and it uses the earnings from its products to produce more products. For research and development the organization relies on grants from the government of India, the United Nations, bilateral donors such as Switzerland and Canada, and private foundations such as the MacArthur Foundation in the United States. "I came to the conclusion a long time ago that most of the research and development in the world, including in the most market-based economy of all, the US, is paid for by the public sector," says Khosla. "Why should the poor have to pay for research? I don't want to pass along the cost of research in the price of our stoves. It's unfair. If nobody's willing to support a radical new idea, then we pay for it ourselves."

"A very wonderful plant"—Zimbabwe

The success of the Jatropha hedge illustrates the synergy that the SL approach seeks to create when it brings in technology from outside to enhance local methods and practices.

In the Zimbabwean village of Mlambaphele, the simple introduction of a bush called Jatropha has enabled herders to expand their livelihood systems to include farming and other forms of income-generation. Their village is located on marginal land, barely suitable for human habitation because of extremely low rainfall. The villagers were forcibly moved there in 1944 as a result of the Land Appropriation Act of 1929, by which the colonial government appropriated the best farming and grazing lands for European farmers. The villagers still live in extreme poverty, but thanks to this adaptive strategy their meager livelihoods are sustainable.

Since 1958, villagers in Mlambaphele have managed to keep their cattle alive, surviving near-drought conditions year after year. The short-term "coping mechanism" they devised in a time of crisis has evolved over four decades into a long-term adaptive strategy. Each June through December, men and boys keep their cattle 10 kilometers away from the village at a place called Mlageni on the banks of the Shashi River on the border with Botswana. While they are there, their village receives its scanty annual rainfall (less than 650 mm), and grasses for grazing are replenished. When the cattle return to the village in December, it is planting season, and they are strong enough to work as draft animals. By the time the cattle go back to the river in June, the grasses there have grown up again. To preserve the environment at Mlageni, the herders do not take their goats to graze there; goats are far more destructive to the environment than cattle and grazing them there would cause serious soil erosion. Furthermore, goats can survive year-round in the village on less water than cattle need. They eat thorny bushes that cattle cannot eat, and they are occasionally given water from bore holes.

Nevertheless, the situation in Mlambaphele is so precarious that cattle, the central feature of their livelihood system, are not consumed for daily survival but simply kept as insurance against disaster. They represent a kind of "savings account" to be drawn on when starvation threatens or when cash is needed for high-priority items such as paying school fees. For food on an everyday basis, goats are milked, slaughtered for their meat, or traded for maize.

In 1994, a simple application of scientific knowledge in Mlambaphele helped increase the productivity and sustainability of the people's livelihood systems. A major problem was the difficulty of protecting crops from the voracious herds of goats in the village. To build fences, the villagers had been cutting down the small trees and thorny bushes on which the goats depended for food, thus destroying needed fodder and degrading the environment. The people's diet lacked vegetables, and malnutrition was rife, but the villagers did not have enough water to grow vegetables. They could not buy them because they had no source of cash. Fortunately, there was a solution that would actually go far toward solving all of these problems sustainably.

The crops could be protected and tree cutting reduced by planting Jatropha Curcas hedges around their fields. "Goats do not eat Jatropha," says Phosiso Sola, an environmental botanist and SL facilitator. "Cattle do not eat Jatropha. But Jatropha produces an oil that can be used for income-generation. In fact, people call it the diesel tree." Furthermore, the oil from Jatropha seeds can be sold for cash, bartered for vegetables, and used by the villagers themselves for cooking and lighting. "And if you process the husks," says Sola with obvious delight, "you actually get very nutritious stock feed, which produces manure containing lots of nitrates for soil fertility. It is a very wonderful plant."

Doing more with less waste

Today, improvements in technology often lead to "downsizing," and to the replacement of human labor by machines. But Jatropha is an example of "upsizing"—increasing productivity, jobs, and economic efficiency while eliminating waste through fairly simple technical interventions that contribute considerably to the productivity and sustainability of the original livelihood.

Traditional economics and business management have taken a wrong turn, ending up in vicious cycle of unemployment, dangerous levels of pollution, and diminishing returns. Economic theory identifies three core input factors that determine the competitiveness of industries: labor, capital, and raw materials. Industry and the stock market have been focusing almost exclusively on squeezing as much as possible out of labor: increasing the output per employee by huge layoffs, causing massive unemployment. They have completely ignored the very real potential of increasing the productivity of raw materials. And not only has the productivity of raw materials been ignored, the vast potential of human knowledge and creativity has been largely overlooked as well.

Gunter Pauli, director of ZERI (the Zero Emissions Research Initiative), an international NGO, claims that by applying generative science—a nonlinear, zero-emission use of natural resources—people can satisfy nearly twenty times more material needs than are currently being supplied, without expecting the earth to produce anything extra and while eliminating waste. Making use of the large proportion of byproducts that are now being thrown away would create a massive job-generating machine. It would also reduce pollution and increase revenues by producing new products all along the line.

"Nature operates in a decentralized manner; practical, pragmatic and with great intelligence," says Pauli, pointing out that everything in nature has a useful purpose, and that nothing is ever wasted. He suggests that in using nature's resources, human beings would do well to imitate the way nature works. "If mankind expects the earth to produce more, the earth may very well collapse," he points out. "But if mankind does more with what the earth produces, then it is likely to succeed in responding to the basic needs for food, water, health care, shelter, energy and jobs—which about one billion people on the planet are lacking today."

Villagers in Namibia, South Africa, Zambia, Zimbabwe, and Tanzania were brewing beer from sorghum and feeding the spent sorghum to their cattle. Thanks to ZERI, they learned to get considerable added value from their beer production. They learned that spent sorghum—while not, in fact, a very nutritious or digestible cattle feed—happens to be an ideal habitat for growing mushrooms, especially when combined with a little water hyacinth (a ubiquitous and hitherto useless "pest weed" that today threatens to choke many bodies of water throughout the tropics). Mineral-rich mushrooms had been absent from the local diet since the destruction of their forest habitat decades ago. Indeed, the medicinal value of mushrooms in strengthening the immune system, enhancing memory, and delaying the aging process has long been recognized, especially in Asia.

But that's not all. Once the mushrooms are harvested, the composted spent sorghum, now enriched and highly nutritious, can be digested easily by cattle. The water hyacinths are fed to earthworms, which in turn are fed to chickens. (According to Pauli, 220 kilograms of earthworms translates into 100 kilograms of chicken meat.) The chicken dung is fed to biogas digesters that produce energy, reducing the need for fuel wood, and convert manure into an improved fertilizer. Another byproduct of the digesters stimulates the growth of algae used in fish farming.

While a total system such as this requires an investment out of most villagers' reach, any one component of the process can be set up at little or no cost and will bring substantial returns. In Suva, Fiji, an entire farm was set up in 1997 according to a similar "cascading" system at a cost of US$30,000. Less than two years later, annual production of fish had reached six tons, bringing in revenues of US$10,000. In addition, annual earnings from chickens, vegetables, fruit, and flowers amount to about $3,500. The farm's director estimates that at this rate the initial investment can be paid off in three to four years. Of course, such models are not always completely replicable; not every community, for instance, has a taste for mushrooms. But the principles these examples illustrate can go far toward increasing productivity, creating jobs, and eliminating waste.

"For people who have no money, I'm interested in what costs zero," says Pauli. In the use of spent sorghum, the only cost is time during the drying process that is necessary before the sorghum is a substrate for mushrooms. With water hyacinth the labor of harvesting is the only cost. "It's a matter of understanding how systems work. If this is understood, materials of zero value are converted into value-added products. Income can be generated with very little capital investment. Jobs can be generated without going through the cycle of needing capital investments."

Pauli also maintains that human creativity must be given free rein if current trends of high pollution and low productivity are to be reversed. He makes the point, for example, that common industrial uses of raw materials are extremely short-sighted and wasteful. "Mankind expects the earth to produce more and more," he says. "Instead, why can't we learn how to do more with what the earth already produces?"

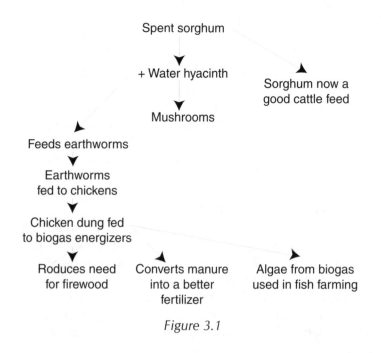

Figure 3.1

Trees

Pauli points out that when trees are felled for paper and pulp, only about 30 percent of their biomass is utilized, while the remaining 70 percent is incinerated. But this 70 percent is a "chemical cocktail" consisting of carbohydrates and lignin, a natural aromatic polymer that can be used as a clean-burning fuel or as an organic additive to cement, rubber, and other composite materials, as well as detergents, adhesives, and glue (as a substitute for epoxy, which is made with cancer-causing formaldehyde). In addition, lignin is a good fertilizer. It enhances soil fertility and stimulates plant development. "When major reforestation projects are undertaken," says Pauli, "or when logging is pursued, it should be carried out with a total use of the biomass of trees in mind." Pauli insists that learning how to use trees for a range of products instead of only one product would reduce pollution, increase revenues, and create jobs.

Sugar cane

Human beings are the only creatures in nature that produce waste no one wants, waste that therefore becomes a pollutant. "In nature a lot of waste is produced, but whatever is waste for one is food for another, and that 'other' is always around," says Pauli. "Nature has organized itself in clusters, and we have to do the same. Instead of looking at one specific product, we need to think of the clusters around that product."

Only a small proportion of sugar cane, for example, is processed for sugar. The remaining biomass—called bagasse—is incinerated as fuel in the sugar-extraction process, increasing pollution and global warming. Using sugar cane primarily as a sweetener is not a smart use of this renewable resource. Dr. Janis Gravitis, Pauli's former colleague at the Institute of Advance Studies at United Nations University in Tokyo, says that his organization (the Latvian State Institute of Wood Chemistry) has found a way to use all of the various components of sugar cane, with virtually "zero emissions."

The main byproduct of sugar cane is syrup-molasses, an excellent raw material for biotechnology or for use as cattle feed. But after separation of the liquid sugar from the canes, 90–95 percent of the remaining bagasse is wasted, burned for fuel in the sugar-cane mill. "Our calculations showed that by using the energy co-generation approach that produces not only steam but also electricity, it is possible to reduce bagasse burning from 10 to 20 percent," says Gravitis. "This 10 to 20 percent of bagasse could be used as a raw material for 'clustering' complementary industries around the sugar mill, manufacturing value-added products."

Products and byproducts of sucrose (sugar)

- Ethanol alcohol
- Furfural
- Vitamins
- Cattle feed
- Glycerin

- Molasses
- Levulinic acid

- Esters and ethers to be used for the synthesis of biodegradable polymers

- Butyl alcohol
- Charcoal
- Fiberboard
- Non-wood paper
- Citric acid

- Bagasse
- An ingredient in soap

Table 3.1

The Institute of Advanced Studies at United Nations University has demonstrated that it is possible to use all the products and byproducts of sugar cane as value-added products without generating emissions. "The industrial cluster is self-sufficient and produces near zero emissions," says Gravitis. "In some countries, such as India and China, bagasse is used as fiber material for non-wood paper. Treating bagasse with steam explosion converts it into cattle feed, which is currently being used by Japanese farmers on Okinawa Island." The potential for paper manufacturing from sugar cane is best of all, since sugar cane matures once a year, while hardwood trees can take as long as 50 years to grow to maturity.

Pauli advocates "clustering" on a much larger scale, as an entirely new approach to industry and the processing of natural resources. He gives several examples that are highly relevant to most developing countries, which are located in the tropics. Based on generative science, clustering involves a zero-emissions, on-site system of producing multiple, value-added products from tropical raw materials. This is a radical departure from the age-old practice of exporting tropical raw materials to be processed in the North, where their unused residues are routinely discarded or burned as wastes.

Seaweed

Seaweed is currently harvested in Namibia, Tanzania, the Philippines, and Indonesia for export to Europe and Japan. Two products are extracted from the seaweed: carrageenan and agar. Both are used in the ice cream industry; agar is also used to create a medium that stimulates the biopropagation of seeds. A third component of seaweed, iodine, is thrown back into the ocean because Europe and Japan have no need of additional iodine supplements in food. Pauli says that in many countries where seaweed grows, some 30 percent of people suffer from iodine deficiency disorders (IDD). According to the World Health Organization, the incidence of IDD is 31.9 percent in Namibia, 34.5 percent in Tanzania, 27.7 percent in Indonesia, and 6.9 percent in the Philippines. So, if the seaweed were processed on site, it would not only create jobs and eliminate one form of pollution, but it would also produce potassium iodide, a product that is desperately needed in many countries rich in seaweed.

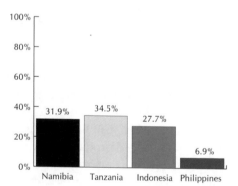

Figure 3.2 Incidence of iodine deficiency disorders as percent of total population

Palm trees

Palm trees are a ubiquitous product of the South. A range of cluster industries can be created to make full use of the biocomponents of palm trees and coconut palms. These include the world's largest potential source of Vitamin E, an antioxidant that strengthens the immune system, but which is currently destroyed in the coconut and palm-oil industries; beta-carotene; fatty acids, used to make biodegradable soaps; sisal, arguably the strongest fiber in nature; furfural, a natural product that can be used in the paint industry as a fungicide; citric acid (valued at US$ 3,000 per ton); and lactic acid.

Palm oil lowers lipoproteins, a potent indicator of heart disease risk, and contain antioxidants such as tocotrienols, tocopherols, and carotenoids. Indeed, says Gravitis, palm oil has such a negligible amount of cholesterol that it is considered cholesterol-free. The Vitamin E in palm oil has an inhibiting effect on the development of tumors. Another major use of the distilled fatty acid in palm oil is in the production of soaps. Palm products produce vegetable-based soap, which is significantly more compatible with the religious beliefs of Hindu, Muslim, and Jewish societies than soaps made from animal byproducts. Also, detergents made from oil palm are readily biodegradable and work extremely well without the use of phosphates, a common source of skin irritation and water pollution. Palm oil detergents even perform well in hard water.

Sisal, a good fiber material, is only a small percentage of the total sisal biomass. Unless sisal production is part of a cascade of industries clustered around the palm tree, sisal production involves considerable waste. "This is a win-win situation," says Pauli. "Through generative science we can raise the productivity of natural resources, generate more revenues, create more jobs, and make health products that will be cheaper and within reach of many more people."

The Latvian State Institute of Wood Chemistry has demonstrated that it is possible to use nearly 100 percent of the biomass waste materials of such plants as oil palms, bamboo, pineapple, and so forth, converting them into value-added products. As a rule, biomass density as well as energy is low in comparison with existing fossil resources. Hence the economic value per unit weight of the materials is also low. But when the target is value-added products, the economic value dramatically increases. Gravitis recommends that the development of biomass conversion technologies or "biorefinery" be based on the principle of local uses in small areas. "About 90 percent of the growth in the world population will occur among people living in countries with traditional village-based ways of life," he says. "Therefore biorefinery technologies should be compact and mobile, oriented to apply in rural areas and generate jobs."

The massive reorganization of industry, trade, and economics that would be necessary to implement Pauli's recommendations on a large scale may seem to relegate his ideas to the realm of fantasy. Techno-economic data confirming all his claims are still being examined, and UNDP, for one, is not prepared to endorse ZERI at this time. It does, however, endorse the principles behind its work, as do a number of development thinkers. As for Pauli, he already meets regularly with executives of major multinational corporations who, he says, are eager to listen to his ideas.

Hope, ingenuity, and sustainable growth—Colombia

Far out on the bare, windswept savannas of Eastern Colombia is a most unlikely community called Gaviotas. It has grown over three decades from nothing more than an idea: the conviction that respect for the environment, combined with an ingenious use of natural resources, can create a self-sustaining community. Today, some five hundred people live, work, and raise their families in Gaviotas, in harmony with nature and with one another. It is an environment where people are encouraged to make full use of their talents, as well as pursuing artistic endeavors such as indigenous music played on locally made instruments, which preserve their cultural heritage. (The story of Gaviotas is documented in *Gaviotas: A Village to Reinvent the World* [White River Junction, Vt.: Chelsea Green Publishing, 1998].)

Gaviotas started out as a kind of incubator for environmentally friendly technologies. Founder Paolo Lugari began inviting engineering students and professors, biologists, and other researchers to this isolated, desolate place during the late 1960s. The inventors were given room and board, but were paid little, if anything, during the early years. Soon local people, with their families, began moving there too. A school was built, then a hospital that offered traditional health care to local Indians, as well as Western medicine to anyone who needed it. Everyone was encouraged to find practical, ecologically efficient ways to solve problems that afflict millions of people around the world, such as the need for clean water, the need for energy, and much, much more.

"People who dare to build a utopia use the same materials available to everyone," a professor of music said one day to Paolo Lugari, "but they find surprising ways to combine them." In 1976 Gaviotas received the first of several grants from UNDP to help the community continue its research and disseminate it outside Colombia.

Some of the technologies that came out of Gaviotas are listed below. The list goes on and on, but all these inventions are not, perhaps, the most remarkable feature of Gaviotas. Since their earliest years on the savanna, Paolo Lugari and his colleagues had tried to find trees—even one tree—that could survive in the thin, crusty, toxic soil. Nothing would grow. Nothing, that is, until they tried Caribbean pines. By 1995 they had planted about six million of them, some of which had grown to a height of forty feet in thirteen years. They learned that tapping the trees for resin to sell on the commercial market could produce a sustainable livelihood for the community. Eventually their resin factory would process twenty tons of top-quality resin per day. But even more remarkable is the fact that in the shade of the pines a tropical rain forest has sprung up, such as has not been seen in this part of Colombia for millennia. Botanists have identified some 245 plant species growing in this brand-new rain forest. In a country where drug trafficking is the major source of wealth, the people of Gaviotas have found in this forest a source of medicinal plants, some of which can be worth as much as US$500 a gram on the international market. The environmental implications for the world of a lush new rain forest growing in a formerly barren spot are tremendous.

Gaviotian technologies
- a blend of local soil and cement used for everything from construction to road paving
- a non-polluting tannery
- gaskets made of palm leaves
- solar refrigerators
- bovine feed supplements made from palm-oil extraction residues
- a hydraulic ram pump used for irrigation
- a hand-operated brick-making machine that produces five hundred bricks a day
- windmills
- solar water-heater panels that even work in the rain (now installed on more than thirty thousand Bogota homes)
- micro-hydro turbines
- biogas generators
- water pumps attached to seesaws and swings and fueled by "kid power"
- an ingenious, nearly effortless way of laying a drainage culvert

- hydroponic vegetable gardens
- environmentally benign water lines, sewage, and septic systems
- a closed-system soil-washer used for making cement
- a non-electric irrigation system using clay to allow plants to water themselves as needed
- a double-action pump connected to an ultra-light windmill
- levers that create and maintain tension on wire fences, even when the gates are open
- a corkscrew manual well-digger
- a parabolic solar grain-dryer
- a rotating-drum peanut-sheller
- an ox-drawn land-grader
- solar pressure-cookers
- methane-fueled stove-top burners
- solar water purifiers that deliver about eight gallons of cool, pure drinking water daily
- a manually powered sleeve pump for drawing pure water from the aquifer
- a complete clean-water-delivery system, installed in six hundred villages as part of a government program
- centrifuge toilets
- remote source pumps that enable people to draw water from a well three hundred meters away without leaving their houses
- a wind-powered irrigator
- a water-distribution center that produces fifteen hundred bags of pure, cold water a day

Gandali, Malawi

In Gandali, clean drinking water was a problem. After much discussion, the people decided not to wait until resources were made available for drilling bore holes. They chose to solve the problem themselves by boiling water for drinking, even though the village is located in a place where there is no firewood. The District Development Office had heard about a simple technology for making energy-efficient, clean-burning briquettes out of fallen leaves, dry grasses, and agricultural residues. After these decompose, they are pounded with a traditional African mortar and pestle, and then compressed by a simple, lever-operated press that produces up to five hundred doughnut-shaped briquettes per day: enough to cook meals or boil drinking water for three hundred people for one day, or for a family of six for forty-eight days. The technology was introduced to Malawi in 1994 by Richard Stanley of Stanlinks, a small NGO based in the United States.

"There were several groups of women making the briquettes," says Stewart Ligomeka, district development officer for Mchinji District, where Gandali is located. "We introduced these women to the village and they began to sell the briquettes at a nearby market. They are affordable. They cost about one-third the price of firewood." Ligomeka estimates that by now the women of Gandali are using these tree-saving briquettes for all their cooking needs. "In fact," he says, "now they want to learn the technology so they can make the briquettes on their own." As district development officer, Ligomeka plans to work with Stanlinks to train people throughout Mchinji District to make, operate, and maintain briquette-making machines, not only as a means of producing cheap fuel and preserving the environment, but as a source of income as well.

When people take the briquettes to market, says Stanley, they are sold immediately. Moreover, using a common, 20–horsepower grain mill instead of pounding the waste materials by hand greatly increases output of briquettes. "All of a sudden you can feed eighteen briquette presses from one maize mill," says Stanley. "Villagers have begun to see this as a real money-making venture."

Sharing information

The development and application of practical, effective, small-scale technologies are clearly escalating. There is an ever-widening web of information networks that describe such technologies and make them available to people in all parts of the world (see Resources herein). For example:

- Paul Harrison's 1987 book, *The Greening of Africa*, describes many simple technologies and applications of scientific knowledge that are being applied more and more to improve environmental conditions and increase agricultural productivity in many parts of Africa.
- Development Alternatives has established a network that provides access to information on sustainable development. It can connect users to the many databases of ENVIS, India's Ministry of Environment and Forests Department of Science and Technology.

- A large network set up by SRISTI (the Society for Research and Initiatives for Sustainable Technologies and Institutions, India) reaches seventy-five countries. The SRISTI-Honey Bee network of grassroots innovators and inventions lists, among other things, local institutions involved in natural resource management projects that are initiated and governed by local people. The SRISTI-Honey Bee network newsletter is published in English and five Indian languages, as well as in Zonkha, the language of Bhutan.

- In Malawi, as part of the government's Sustainable Livelihoods program, a multi-track communications system is being set up. It will describe technologies that have been applied successfully in the local context, with simple instructions on how such technologies can be implemented. The system will be used to access information about new technologies and to learn about experiences with technology in other districts, reports UNDP resident representative Terence Jones.

If the livelihood systems of the poorest people throughout the world are to be made more sustainable and more productive, science and technology must be made more widely available to everyone. Ready access to information—especially at the community level—is crucial. "For every one local solution documented and shared," says Anil K. Gupta of India's SRISTI-Honey Bee network, "there exist perhaps thousands of others which remain to be documented, experimented with, and disseminated."

——— Tips and Lessons Learned ———

♦ Technology should improve the productivity of a community's assets, enhance capabilities, and provide for new livelihood opportunities for the poor. It should be sustainable in an environmental and socioeconomic sense; that is, it should promote equality in society; empower communities, especially vulnerable groups; and link communities and relevant stakeholders in similar circumstances through networks.

♦ We should not expect the earth to produce more; instead, people should do more with what the earth produces.

♦ Nature is able to utilize wastes and pests by incorporating them into the natural ecosystem.

♦ Each adopted technology should add incremental value to livelihoods.

♦ The "appropriateness" of a technology must be measured by how well it satisfies the needs of the client, and with what success it takes into account the opportunities and constraints of the production and marketing processes.

♦ Technology development should emphasize the importance of establishing links between indigenous knowledge and outside scientific knowledge.

♦ SL conditions vary from region to region due to agro-ecological differences. Local biodiversity must be considered when identifying the mix of technologies, catalysts, and change agents that will best address a given situation.

♦ Examine how modern technologies can strengthen traditional technologies, and how traditional technologies could enhance modern approaches.

♦ Build on what is already in a community—don't reinvent the wheel. Build partnerships even with organizations that may also be competitors in other areas.

♦ The identification of new technologies should be subjected to SL simulation models.

♦ Capacity for developing technological solutions to promote Sustainable Livelihoods can be built through small- and medium-sized businesses and microenterprises.

4

Investments and Financial Services

Synergy: The interaction of two or more agents or forces so that their combined effect is greater than the sum of their individual effects.

—*American Heritage Dictionary*

Long-range economic, social, and environmental stability can, and does, come about as a result of the synergy of elements that make up the Sustainable Livelihoods approach. As discussed in chapter 1, sustainable livelihoods are characterized by resilience—the ability to cope with and recover from shocks and stresses—as well as ecological integrity, economic efficiency, and social equity. The SL paradigm shows how these four elements can work together to create sustainable livelihoods. Yet the building blocks that produce these elements are not unique to the SL approach; they are well-known development techniques. Participation and empowerment foster self-confidence and initiative; access to science and appropriate technology promotes economic efficiency and ecological integrity; investments and financial services promote resilience and nurture economic efficiency; and good governance and policy set the stage for social equity, which in turn strengthens the sustainable interplay of all the other elements.

Building the building blocks

In Malawi and many other parts of the world, the building blocks of traditional development are not yet firmly in place. The job of development practitioners consists not only in creating the synergy of these elements that lead to sustainable livelihoods. Sometimes it is important to work on the building blocks themselves, the traditional activities that development agencies normally undertake. The Malawi program's participation and empowerment phase enabled the people to identify interventions in the area of science and technology that would benefit them: the use of organic rather than chemical fertilizers, the planting of drought-resistant trees, education, training, investments and financial services to help them establish viable business enterprises. While these building blocks of development were being constructed, the synergy that produces sustainable livelihoods was occurring as well.

When enterprises are launched or credit is extended in keeping with social equity and ecological integrity from the start, the outcome is much more likely to be livelihood systems that are sustainable, that is, equitable, efficient, environmentally benign, and resilient. On the other hand, as B. T. Costantinos, team leader of UNDP's SL program in Malawi, affirms, "Once economic growth goes off in its own direction, correcting the damage caused to the environment may require another project aimed at environmental rehabilitation. So it is important to design economic development and growth programs in such a way that they are environmentally sustainable from the beginning. That's the kind of synergy that's necessary."

Unfortunately, in many of the mature economies of industrialized nations, development has taken place without this synergy among ecological integrity, economic efficiency, and social equity. Where these elements have not established a cohesive pattern, they have tended to work in opposition to one another. While political leaders in the United States, for example, are aware of the importance of taking steps to preserve or restore global environmental soundness, perceived economic interests have so far prevented them from ratifying a number of global conventions on the environment for fear of limiting economic growth. But when patterns of development include from the start the elements of economic efficiency and ecological integrity, such conflicts need not occur.

"There is no future for poor people unless they can make a lot more money than they are making today and save something so that they can invest in productive capacity tomorrow," says Ashok Khosla, director of Development Alternatives in India. This is where programs such as the renowned Grameen Bank in Bangladesh have fallen short. Although such programs provide much-needed credit for small businesses, most borrowers remain in subsistence or even mere survival mode. Credit is very important, of course, but technologies must be introduced, productivity increased, and the ability of people to generate and save money must be enhanced so they can invest it for further improvements in productivity. "The Grameen approach does not allow for that," says Khosla. "It only enables people to continue doing what they were doing before. Development implies progress. A program based on credit liberates people from the grip of the moneylenders, but they still remain chained to the bank."

What is needed, therefore, is the micro-macro linkage that expands income-generating activities through the marriage of "outside" to "inside" technology, enabling the poor to move beyond the subsistence level to greater productivity, while maintaining environmental sustainability. While recognizing the benefits the Grameen Bank has produced for its desperately poor population, there is a tendency to view Grameen as a universal panacea.

The complex issue of credit for women

It has become fashionable in recent years to think of microcredit programs, especially those designed for women (as most of them are) in almost messianic terms, as "quick fixes" for both poverty and the subjection of women. But the issue is far more complex. Participants at the International Working Group on Sustainable Livelihoods held in Pearl River, New York, in November 1997, noted that increased access to capital has been linked by studies to greater political participation and bargaining power for women in the home, and to greater expenditures on food, health, and education. Anecdotal evidence of the benefits of providing credit to women abounds. Access to credit in the form of revolving funds for women, for example, has long been a home-grown feature in many communities around the world.

A great deal of excitement has been generated by the apparently dramatic results obtained from providing microcredit to micro-entrepreneurs who are women. This is due to the work of organizations like the Self-Employed Women's Association in Ahmedabad, India; the Working Women's Forum in Madras, India; Pro Mujer in Bolivia (founded in the late 1980s); Finca, Accion International; and the Grameen Bank in Bangladesh; as well as countless other credit programs for women around the world. A number of impressive results have been reported. Poor women have shown themselves to be excellent credit risks, repaying their loans on time at a rate of at least 97 percent. Women also tend to spend all their earnings on the welfare of their families.

Through credit programs, many women around the world who are the main breadwinners for their families are able to run small businesses successfully for the first time, without becoming mired in debt to rapacious moneylenders. All this has added to the euphoria surrounding the issue of credit for women. However, credit does not necessarily mean empowerment. "There has been an assumption that giving women financing would automatically empower them," says Sarah Murison, senior technical advisor to UNDP's Gender and Development Programme. "But although a number of organizations claim to deliver credit and empowerment in the same package, it is virtually impossible for one organization to achieve both of these very different goals at once."

Attempts simultaneously to deliver microfinance and to give women opportunities to meet together and discuss issues that would empower them have not been taking place. "To be a loan officer requires very different skills from those of a community development worker," says Murison. "They are different functions and should be conducted separately. The loan officer, for example, does not have the skills that are necessary to enable women to talk among themselves when they have never been accustomed to doing so—especially women from different social strata within the same village."

The hope was that women would be empowered at no cost, that they would "pay" for their own empowerment through the interest on the microfinancing. But this is not the case. It is incorrect to assume that combining microfinance with empowering activities is possible. If each function were given equal priority and carried out systematically and carefully, Murison states, it would be possible, but there may be costs to the rate of return on the loan.

"Why is it that women are better at repaying loans than men?" asks Murison. "It may have to do with their relative lack of power as social actors. They have more respect for authority, they are more obedient, and so on. If these suppositions are true, the high repayment rate is dependent on their low status—on their disempowerment." It would therefore follow that if an agency's first priority were to receive the highest possible repayment rates from its clients, it would be counterproductive to empower women. This applies to the very poorest of poor women. There is evidence that when women take out slightly larger loans, their repayment rate is about the same as men's. "A key thing that is not often in the literature is this: In order to get these high repayment rates, loan officers go to the households and squeeze it out of the women. They do it with threats: The woman will not get another loan. She'll be humiliated, and so on." The women are easier to find because their businesses are often based at home, whereas the men could be anywhere. So even if not based on the disempowerment of women directly, the fact that it is easier to collect the loans from women may indicate that the disempowerment of women is very important.

There is also the question of whether or not doing better financially confers a degree of empowerment on women. There is not a direct correlation. In some studies women report that their husbands are more accepting of them and now recognize that they have a role to play, which is very encouraging. However, this may be due to factors other than access to credit, such as particular cultural situations in which wives are not totally oppressed. The connection between credit and empowerment needs to be demonstrated more consistently across the board. In very many cases there may be improvements in the situation of women if they are bringing income into the households. But the key question, Murison says, is whether microfinance does in fact lead to increases in income.

Then there is the question of who actually uses the loan money—the woman or her husband. "It is well known that in fact the money often goes straight into the hands of men," says Murison, "and they use it for their businesses. Very often the women are sent by their husbands to get the loans. This would not necessarily be a bad thing if the family income were equally shared within the household." But it has also been documented in many countries that men tend to spend their income on their own amusements rather than on their families. "So it is very important," says Murison, "that the money goes to the women and that it generates income for women—but it may not."

It has not been unequivocally proven that credit for women actually results, in a majority of cases, in increases in women's income. Slippages occur, and in some cases women borrow from other sources of credit—other NGOs or even traditional moneylenders—to pay back the loans from their primary credit program. "In this case, the process is disempowering," Murison says. "Women report that they work a lot harder now that they have loans." It is well known, for example, that in Africa women take out loans for agricultural purposes and repay them by brewing beer. They need the loans to grow more food, but the credit does not actually improve their income. It depletes their income, even though they do have more food. If they did not have to pay back their loans, they would brew the beer and sell it for added income. Credit is by no means a panacea.

Credit for women: Summary of key points
These five key points on the issue of credit for women need to be understood:
1. Credit does not necessarily lead to improved income.
2. If there is improved income, this probably does improve the status of women. However, it may not necessarily do so when their low status derives from factors other than income.
3. The method of delivery of the financial service may be inherently disempowering, because getting high rates of return is not automatic. It often involves putting pressure on women.
4. Credit can only pay for empowerment if there is a distinct linear relationship between credit, improved income, and improved status. Such a relationship has not yet been fully demonstrated.
5. It may be possible to demonstrate a correlation between extremely low status and high repayment rates.

—Sarah Murison,
UNDP senior technical advisor for Gender and Development

Flexibility and diversification

Some studies have shown that participation in microfinance or microenterprise programs has actually tended to increase women's work loads, while not necessarily resulting in improved nutrition or better quality of life as defined by the women themselves. For example, if a woman's new business requires that she keep her children out of school to help her pay back a loan, she may not find the business to be very beneficial to family well-being or to her children's future, which tend to be her top priorities. In addition, researchers have found that an emphasis on growth-oriented investments at the expense of other factors often bypasses the most vulnerable populations and may indirectly disadvantage women. This is true, for example, of investments in cash crops that may require additional work from women while the earnings accrue only to men, who, as noted before, usually do not spend them on the needs of the family.

All these findings point to a basic truth: microfinance programs must be guided by, and tailored to, the needs and the proven adaptive strategies of the poor themselves, both as a starting point and as a means of evaluating success. Furthermore, investment strategies must be designed in such a way that they strengthen each phase of the employment-generation cycle, including promotion, production, and marketing. And, especially for the most destitute populations where food security is a top priority (such as Ethiopia and Malawi), investment strategies should also emphasize the development of sustainable local financial institutions responsive to local needs.

People should be encouraged to articulate their needs and preferences according to their individual talents, experiences, and circumstances. Poor people, particularly women, often become adept at judging local markets and the potential viability of various income-generating activities, for without such astuteness they could not survive. While some investment strategies tend to favor certain livelihood systems, others may have the effect of marginalizing them. For example, income-generation schemes often focus on income growth, financial capital, expansion strategies, and measuring success with exogenously developed indicators. At the same time, they may tend to ignore such factors as social capital, long-term natural resource preservation, and risk reduction.

To promote sustainable livelihoods, therefore, a broader conceptual framework for investments is needed. In other words, emergency resources, expanded skills training, appropriate technology, and the nurturing of environmental resources should all be part of the investment mix. Investment schemes should include, but not be limited to, employment generation and microfinance services. At the national level, high priority should be placed on investments that support livelihoods, such as social investments in non-formal and formal education, health, emergency aid and relief, as well as political participation, sound local governance, and community-based programs that restore and preserve the environment. Changes also must be brought about in policies that have a negative effect on the livelihood systems of the poor, such as land reform or the lack of it. In other words, an SL approach to investments demands the same diversity and flexibility as those found in the actual livelihood systems and adaptive strategies of the people themselves. Moreover, financial services should promote ongoing diversification and flexibility in people's livelihood systems, enabling them constantly to adapt, expand, and respond to new circumstances.

Financial thinking tends to focus on financial capital, using economics as the only valid yardstick for measuring success, while ignoring other, even more valuable forms of capital such as social, human, and natural capital. If natural capital is valued, for example, environmental soundness will not be sacrificed for short-term financial rewards. And conversely, a short-term forgoing of income may result in greater social equity and long-term social capital returns. Indeed, economists could learn much from observing the household strategies of resource management among the poor themselves, where nothing is wasted and careful use is made of every commodity.

The current focus on microenterprises is often based on one-dimensional thinking and often fails to take into account the reality that income-generation activities are only part of a complex web of interrelated activities taking place in the household, the community, and the market. To meet more appropriately the specific needs of a wide range of individuals living in diverse situations, investment strategies can be thought of as belonging to one of three categories: survival strategies, stability strategies, or accumulation strategies.

Survival strategies

People who are surviving in marginal situations—such as those living in fragile ecosystems, post-conflict or resettlement areas, remote rural areas, or urban squatter settlements—do not initially require growth-oriented financial strategies. Above all, they need risk-reduction strategies with a heavy emphasis on social investments such as health care and education. Microfinance programs may be inappropriate in areas where there is no access to markets and no infrastructure for basic needs. In these cases, the public sector and/or donor agencies should target investments to support the people's traditional coping mechanisms, as well as health, education, social mobilization, and strengthening civil society organizations.

The principles of SL have been applied in the Zimbabwean village of Mlambaphele, which exists outside of the scope of financial services, especially banking. Moreover, a focus on one form of livelihood—cattle—has left the people dangerously vulnerable. Turning to friends and family for financial help in times of crisis—usually to those who have moved away and have a more or less reliable source of income—has been the most common practice when disaster strikes.

In Mlambaphele, wealth is measured in livestock. People must pool their primary resource, their cattle, as collateral security for taking out loans from government agencies (currently being privatized), such as the Agricultural Finance Corporation (AFC) or the Cold Storage Commission (CSC). However, the requirement that prospective borrowers offer collateral tends to reinforce poverty, because farmers with no cattle to offer are ineligible for loans.

The agencies extend loans of four to five heifers per person to groups of ten people. But the system compromises the promotion of indigenous breeds that are more drought-tolerant and better suited to local conditions. Foreign breeds are promoted by the agencies because they grow faster, calving within the three-year loan cycle, and they fetch higher prices, although they also have high mortality rates and do not adapt well to the very low rainfall in the area. Local breeds have lower birth rates and often do not breed within the three years of the loan cycle, but they are far more drought-tolerant. For the most part, these loans of foreign breeds are used for cattle-fattening projects and for steers to build up herds. During the severe drought of 1992, most of the cattle in the area died—both the livestock bought with loan money and the cattle that had been used as collateral security. The loans were canceled as bad debts by the AFC. While the idea behind this credit system was to enable people to rebuild their herds after depletion due to natural calamities, more carefully designed loan policies that encourage the breeding of indigenous herds might have prevented disaster in the first place.

In such areas of extreme poverty the synergy between technology and finance can be especially dynamic. The people of Mlambaphele are outside the loop of modern financial services, and lack of cash in the local economy puts them at a disadvantage for several reasons. First, their "savings," in the form of livestock, are highly vulnerable to low levels of rainfall and the high mortality rates of a particular breed of cattle. Second, the community's only source of credit is the system of loans of heifers, whereby the people had to offer their existing herds as collateral. Third—and perhaps most important—without an inflow of cash on a daily basis the people had no means to purchase items and produce that were needed for family nutrition, such as vegetables, which could not be grown in the village for lack of water. The introduction of the Jatropha hedge, discussed in chapter 3, not only protected crops from wandering ruminants but also provided cash income for the local women. It diversified local livelihood systems by planting the seeds of new businesses, improving family diets, giving women buying power, and bringing them into the money economy.

Case study—
REST's financial services and resilience, Ethiopia

Whether or not they empower women, financial services such as credit and savings are generally recognized as important steps in promoting economic self-sufficiency and resilience. This resilience is the ability to recover from shocks and stresses such as the chronic drought, war, and environmental degradation that have occurred over the last few decades in disaster-prone regions such as Ethiopia's province of Tigray.

Tigray is a mountainous, arid, embattled place, just recently emerging from the devastation of seventeen years of civil war. The Relief Society of Tigray (REST)—which is supported by donor agencies and private foundations in the international community, including Norway, the United States, Canada, Japan, and Australia—is working to promote sustainable human development, first by building a firm foundation of food security in a region chronically afflicted by famine.

REST's food security initiative has two dimensions, or pillars: availability of food, and access to food. Its credit and savings program was introduced in 1994 to address the issue of poor people's access to food. REST's credit and savings scheme has six main objectives: (1) to boost agricultural production; (2) to diversify socioeconomic activities; (3) to create employment at the household level (petty trade and small-scale manufacturing); (4) to promote the creation of different types of services; (5) to liberate the people from the exploitation of traditional moneylenders, who were charging an interest rate of 74 to 125 percent per year; and (6) to introduce a culture of savings and investment in order to promote resilience by helping people build their own economic cushions or "safety nets" as a means of withstanding and recovering from the shocks and stresses that continue to plague this drought-prone region.

With a highly decentralized structure, REST's 12 main branches and 109 sub-branches cover most of Tigray (population 3.5 million). As of October 1997, more than 137 million birr (US$19.5 million) had been distributed in loans. REST works closely with the Ministry of Agriculture, which provides agricultural extension services to its clients, and with the Ministry of Trade, women's organizations, and farmers' associations that offer other business-related services to borrowers. REST's loan repayment rate is 97.5 percent.

Clients are divided into two main categories. Some 230,000 borrowers take out loans to pay for a package of agricultural inputs (selected or improved seeds, fertilizer, pesticides, and livestock, such as poultry or bees for beekeeping) in order to increase farm yields. In 1998, it was expected to reach a total of 320,000 borrowers with this service. The second group of clients number about 130,000. Their loans are used for business activities: trade, manufacturing, and services, with larger loans for crop production, livestock development, and horticulture.

The range and diversity of economic activities that have been strengthened by REST's credit program include trading cattle, sheep and goats; selling cereals and vegetables; shopkeeping; barbering; tailoring; preparing and selling local food and drink. Craft-based activities include pottery, basket-making, goldsmithing, spinning, weaving, tannery, carpentry, and metal work. And in the service category there are local tea shops, local drink shops, and food shops.

Some 35.5 percent of REST's clients are women. According to REST's director in Ethiopia, Assefa Tekleweyni, "Our policy is that our clients should be 60 percent women, 40 percent men, but we have not reached this yet. The main problem is that when you go deeper into the rural areas, where women traditionally do not take initiatives outside the home, the number of women who participate decreases. As you get closer to the urban places, 97 percent of our clients are women." But as a whole, Tigray is an overwhelmingly rural province. Only 15 percent of REST's clients live in urban areas.

Haimanot Kebedew is one of REST's 360,000 clients. She is 39 years old, divorced with four children, and lives in a particularly remote and impoverished area of Tigray. To support her children she opened a small tea shop about three years ago, borrowing money at an exorbitant interest rate from local moneylenders—the "rich people" in her village. She and her children barely had enough to eat, and most of her earnings went to pay her debt. She could not afford to send her children to school but had to send them out to work instead. The boys tended livestock for nearby farmers and the girls fetched water for neighbors for a small fee.

Then, two years ago, Mrs. Kebedew heard that REST had opened a credit and savings scheme in her area. She signed up and took out two successive loans, the first for 800 birr (US$114) and the second for 1,000 birr (US$143), to expand her business. The interest rate is 12.5 percent per year. The only collateral she had to come up with was to join a group of six other borrowers, who encourage one another in their business activities and in repaying their loans on time.

Since then, her financial situation has changed. "With the income from my tea room I have been able to build a new house," she says. "And I was able to buy more supplies and diversify my business, so that now I prepare food in my tea room as well." Most important to Mrs. Kebedew is that her children's labor is no longer needed. She is now able to feed them well and to send them to school wearing decent clothes and shoes. In the two years since she took her first loan from REST, she has repaid her loans on time and has accumulated a total of 8,500 birr (US$1,214) in profits, which she spent on her new house, a bed and chair, and cooking utensils. She has also put 2,000 birr (US$286) into a savings account—a comforting hedge against disaster in a precarious environment.

So far, REST's 360,000 clients have managed to save a total of 50 million birr (US$7.14 million). This means that when drought struck again in early 1998, these people were able to withstand the shock. By drawing on their savings they managed to keep their farms and small businesses afloat. Even after withdrawals for emergency needs, net savings of 29 million birr (US$4.14 million) remained.

"Generally, we are reaching the poorest of the poor," says Tekleweyni. Like Sustainable Livelihoods programs, REST believes in building on the activities people were already engaged in. "We give them credit so that they can be more productive. What the credit does right away is to increase the activities they have been doing, and it also helps them reclaim what they have lost." For example, many people had lost their oxen (the equivalent of a tractor) or homes during periods of drought. "A house can be a production factory, or a tea room, or a shop. With the savings, new homes and livestock have been purchased."

REST is aware of the pitfalls involved when credit becomes an end in itself, and it has begun to look beyond credit to develop business services that promote innovation among its clients. "Promoting new kinds of businesses is our immediate priority now," says Tekleweyni. There is concern that credit alone tends to be used to maintain existing activities rather than expanding into new, more sophisticated, higher value-added areas. "We want to help people move into these new areas," he says, "otherwise the existing markets will become saturated. We are thinking of how to give people access to improved technology, raw materials, skills training, and information on market opportunities"—in other words, a synergy of key elements that promotes sustainable livelihoods.

Case study—
Financial strategies in Malawi's SL program

The three components, or building blocks, of the Sustainable Livelihoods program in Malawi are food security, natural resource management, and enterprise development. In addition, a fourth component, called a program-wide, cross-sectoral support document, is designed to cut across these three elements and create a synergy among them. The PAPSL process falls under this fourth heading, which empowers communities and promotes local "ownership" of development activities. Also included is the multi-track communications system, which fosters social equity, good governance, and democracy by providing the means for all stakeholders at the local and national levels and in public and private sectors to communicate openly among themselves about all issues relating to economic, social, and political development. The idea is that natural resource management and enterprise development, working together, build food security in a way that is economically efficient and environmentally sustainable. The largest area of expenditure will be for capacity building of beneficiaries at the household level and training of field staff and extension workers to serve the target communities. The purpose is to empower individuals to solve their own problems and carry out their own development plans. Once the groups of households have identified a specific need, SL facilitators must help to provide for that need by helping the households develop a certain type of capacity. Resources above and beyond financial resources should support this effort. If the target groups, the households, need specific strengths, then they should get training services so that they can acquire these strengths.

In the village of Nyamawende, skills training, enterprise development, and income-generation were identified by the villagers as solutions to community problems, such as malnutrition, low income, and the overburdening of women. Among the steps to be taken to solve these problems, the people listed business training and help with starting business ventures, such as raising poultry for the sale of eggs and chickens, as well as training in such skills as carpentry, tinsmithing, carving, basket-making, bricklaying, pottery, black-smithing, painting, art, and tailoring.

A number of local organizations that provide business training and promote small enterprise developments (such as the National Association of Business Women) visited the six SL villages in Mchinji District in June 1998 to discuss with the people the kinds of enterprises that would be most likely to succeed there. "We looked at the village assessment reports and asked these experts to say what they though was feasible in those areas—bearing in mind that we did not want supply-driven activities; we wanted demand-driven activities," says Peter Kulemeka, UNDP's SL Program Manager in Malawi. The business organizations planned to assess such factors as accessibility to markets; the need for financial services, such as credit; and the various kinds of skills and business training required.

In the case of Nyamawende, proximity to the district headquarters and location along a main road are assets likely to enhance business opportunities. But other communities involved in the SL program are far more remote. "The idea there is to involve other institutions that can identify useful activities in the area," says Kulemeka. For example, if people are growing potatoes or yams in one area and do not have a market for them, the facilitators would expect to find out what sort of assistance they can provide, perhaps by encouraging the people to form an association or cooperative that could hire, or even purchase, a vehicle to link up with a market elsewhere.

The Malawi Industrial Research and Technology Development Centre, which works on applied technology, also has studied the village reports. This organization has been examining such areas as energy-saving technology and commercial food processing that would reduce the amount of waste and maximize the nutritional value of foodstuffs, such as soybeans, which were formerly grown for sale and not eaten by the villagers themselves. According to Peter Kulemeka, it has prepared a proposal that covers seven areas for possible intervention in these villages. "And we're also involving the universities, those which may have some technical knowledge which would be viable in these areas," says Kulemeka.

But perhaps the institution with the broadest outreach for enterprise development activities and business development programs is the Small Enterprise Development Organisation of Malawi. One of its branches provides microfinance, actual lines of credit needed to set up business ventures. "We want to challenge a number of key specialized individuals in Malawi and say, 'Look at these village reports. What do you think can be done?'" says Kulemeka. "We don't just want to promote business in a traditional way; we're trying to be innovative and do something that can be meaningful to the people." In the firestorm of enthusiasm that has arisen in recent years over the issue of microfinance, one of the experts who warn against viewing credit as a panacea is Jose Garson of the United Nations Capital Development Fund (UNCDF). He points out that what people really need is a variety of banking services, including credit and savings. "Microfinance organizations can develop credit and savings services," he says, "but they can provide no solution to the excess liquidity that exists at most local levels, because they themselves have to rely on banks to operate and get their cash transformed into deposits and reinvested in the economy." He also points out that since microfinance organizations do not belong to the banking "grid," they are not interconnected among themselves. As a result, he says, "they can only operate in isolation within their own areas, with no possibility to transfer funds in or out of this area." Accessibility to banks, he insists, is the answer.

But in most cases poor farmers and artisans find it virtually impossible to obtain access to the services banks provide. Cultural, educational, and social barriers stand in their way, together with an acute sense of disempowerment. Peter Kulemeka believes that "an institution is needed that stands between the bank and the final beneficiaries—perhaps some solidarity groups who would be the main mechanism for receiving credit and making savings. These groups must be allowed some flexibility to do transactions among themselves." The essence of a microfinance program is to have such "village banks" operating and to make sure that they receive adequate input and "backstopping" from another layer of institutions or NGOs.

An organization such as the National Association of Business Women might be interested in financing enterprises in Nyamawende. "The plan as of now would be to ask the commercial banks to on-lend to these institutions, who would in turn on-lend to groups in the village," Kulemeka says. "We're looking at UNCDF to act as a guarantor for the money transferred from the commercial banks to the institutions which lend to the beneficiaries." In addition, UNCDF and UNDP have each provided US$13.3 million (as well as technical assistance) to Malawi's Governance and Development Management Program to fund the Action Plans drawn up by villages in Mchinji District. These plans can include investments for enterprise development in

the form of seed money from NGOs or loans from institutions carrying out microfinance in Mchinji District.

Furthermore, the SL program has set up District Development
Funds (DDFs) in six districts in Malawi. These funds, says UNDP
resident representative Terence Jones, are designed to handle the
various amounts of money needed to implement community-based
Action Plans from as many as eighty donors at one time. Seventy
percent of DDF funds are allocated as grants for community-driven
projects, such as the funding of village Action Plans, and some projects
initiated at the district level. The remaining 30 percent of DDF funds
is allocated for projects initiated by the District Executive Committee and addresses district-wide issues such as the environment or
AIDS. "The government has established the District Development
Fund so resources can be made available at the District level. They
don't have to go through central government," says Terence Jones.

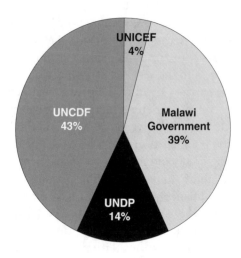

Figure 4.1 Total allocation to the six DDFs

The total allocation of funding to the six DDFs as of the fifth cycle of
the UNDP program is US$1.4 million. The money has been used to
construct eighty-one school blocks, thirty-seven teachers' houses, sixteen bridges, three health posts, one maize mill, five "under-five"
clinic shelters, three postal agencies, two hostels, two postal staff
houses, five police staff houses, two public conveniences, two dental
clinics, and one homecraft shelter. It has also been used to dig five
shallow wells, one tube well, and sixteen bore holes, and to rehabilitate

148 existing bore holes. It has launched two AIDS awareness campaigns, one hospital nutrition program and two water and sanitation programs; and set up one tree nursery.

Eventually the plan is that district development officers, and even villagers, will be able to use a computerized network in the district office to look up technologies that might meet their needs, or to hook up directly with a wide range of potential donors for the funding of specific projects, such as the digging of bore holes or the building of the nursery schools outlined in Nyamawende's Action Plans.

A wide diversity of potential investors is as desirable as a diversity of investment services and strategies. Experts say that investment strategies should integrate public and private sector, community and international commitments. At the same time, community involvement and participation, the seeds of which were sown in Nyamawende by the PAPSL process in 1997, are important elements in creating a sense of local ownership for livelihood-enhancing investments.

How will success be measured in Nyamawende? It should be measured according to indicators that are meaningful to the people. In general, systems of monitoring should be flexible enough to allow for variations across geographical areas and households. Gender analysis, qualitative tools, and participatory approaches should be important complements to existing methods for understanding seasonal changes, the ability to deal with risk, and the relative role of financial services.

The report of the International Working Group on Sustainable Livelihoods (November 1997) concludes that international organizations should attempt to build on existing research and on practices that may already be operating effectively in support of livelihood strategies in different contexts. A number of organizations have made important contributions in the area of financial strategies. The International Food Policy Research Institute and the World Bank have both conducted research on rural microfinance and rural financial strategies. The AIMS project of USAID has developed a comprehensive set of papers on measuring impact, household conceptual frameworks, and risk. SEEP, a network of microfinance/microenterprise practitioners, CARE, and Women's World Banking have each produced a number of manuals for use by microfinance organizations; the tools and methodologies these contain include participatory and qualitative approaches, such as social wealth ranking and subsector analysis. The Microfinance Network has produced publications on policy issues, regulation, and supervision and a Microenterprise

Policy Institute has been established in Bolivia to address policy issues in that country at the national level.

In Malawi, a number of international donors have come forward to supply the building blocks of traditional development initiatives. For example, Oxfam UK has offered to co-fund activities in a new district, Mulanje. And the director of an Irish-based NGO, Self-Help International, proposed that his organization would fund the Action Plans that villagers would draw up in yet another district, Chiradzulu. Once a sound basis for local ownership of development is established, local people themselves make plans that cover economic, environmental, and social initiatives—the essential elements of the synergy that promotes sustainable livelihoods.

"The beauty of being cross-thematic," says UNDP's Thierry Lemaresquier, "is that there are many NGOs on the ground, especially in countries like Malawi. In applying this approach, the chances are increased that other donors will see how they can contribute. It opens up all kinds of opportunities."

—— Tips and Lessons Learned ——

♦ A generalized, "one size fits all" approach to microfinance does not work.

♦ Those considered the poorest of the economically active need stability strategies. These households and communities are often involved in subsistence, small-holder agriculture, street vending, petty trade, and commerce. Investment schemes for these clients should include stabilizing mechanisms such as precautionary savings programs, as well as access to working capital, consumption credit, and insurance schemes.

♦ Collateral should be flexible and non-exclusionary, taking the form of small, movable assets, livestock, or solidarity groups, whichever is most appropriate for the clients.

♦ An approach is needed to smooth consumption, increase the capacity to bear risk, and enable the poor to invest in assets for long-term security.

♦ Although basic communication, financial, and market infrastructures for this population do exist, gaps in these networks must be addressed.

♦ Social investments should include support for entrepreneurial skills, marketing, and training.

♦ Economic activities should build on local technologies and support linkages between rural and urban activities. For example, an investment scheme could help rural producers establish links with commercial vendors and markets in urban areas.

♦ Savings schemes are important as insurance against hard times, but more emphasis should be placed on technological support, vocational training, and education. When these are in place, flexible financial services such as microfinance have greater potential to support people's economic strategies.

♦ The private sector may be willing to play a more active role in supporting the activities of this group of clients.

5

Governance and Policy

Perhaps the most important prerequisite for creating sustainable livelihoods, and for achieving sustainable development, is good and accessible government.

—Ashok Khosla

Governments need reform

In November 1997, the International Working Group on Sustainable Livelihoods compiled a report on policy and governance as key elements required to promote the economic efficiency, ecological integrity, and social equity that make up sustainable livelihoods. The report makes clear that the greatest challenge to attaining sustainable livelihoods lies in the weaknesses of many developing country governments—particularly in Africa.

Good governance that supports sustainable livelihoods must be credible and predictable. Its macro policies must be informed by micro realities and characterized by fiscal prudence. Such policies must be pro-poor; that is, they must empower and benefit the poor and, wherever possible, they must be generated through the participation of the poor. At the local level, sensitivity to gender and power must inform such policies, and they must be designed to improve the livelihoods of the poor.

Characteristics of unsound governance:
- stagnant, inept, and unresponsive bureaucracies
- inconsistent administrative machinery
- corrupt institutions

- a lack of transparency in fiscal affairs
- a lack of commitment to upholding the constitution or bill of rights, where they exist, and a reluctance to formulate such norms and standards where they do not exist.

If government budgets are not transparent, governments can, and often do, spend national resources to build large military forces rather than to provide education, health care, infrastructure (particularly in the rural areas), and other services that would support sustainable livelihoods and thus alleviate—if not eradicate—poverty.

Most policy and legislation in most countries is anti-poor. If it were not, we would not have the levels of poverty that we do have. So removing those policies that are obstacles to true development is the key. Using the Sustainable Livelihoods approach to do this can be quite effective.

—Thierry Lemaresquier
Director of UNDP's Social Development and Poverty Elimination Division

Many governments need help in building systems, policies, and processes that promote and support sustainable livelihoods. One way to do this is to encourage a shift from the compartmentalized, sectoral approach to development, to a more integrated, multi-stakeholder, holistic approach that creates a synergy among the economic, ecological, and social dimensions of sustainable development.

In order to promote sustainable livelihoods, therefore, governments must be sensitive to what is actually happening to people's livelihoods. Leonard Joy is a consultant on governance with UNDP who, with Robert Chambers at the Institute for Development Studies, Sussex University, UK, was among the first to focus development thinking on the concept of livelihoods. "Monitoring unemployment is not the same as asking, 'Are people able to provide for themselves?'" says Joy. "Livelihood is not an optional extra. It's the very basis of survival, of society, and of economic stability. Unless the causes of disrupted livelihoods or lack of livelihood are addressed, attempts to secure sustainable livelihoods will be fragmented and will not eradicate poverty in any meaningful way or on a large scale."

The goal of supporting sustainable livelihoods through policy management is to ensure that there is productive, fulfilling, healthy, non-exploitative, non-coercive, non-dependent, environmentally sustainable work that provides for all to be self-supporting at an acceptable material level of living and for all to be assimilated fully into the economy and society.

Society as ecosystem

Several development thinkers today find it useful to regard society as an ecosystem. The metaphor is intended to liken society to a living organism in which each part or member has a crucial role to play, helps sustain the whole, and lives in an interdependent relationship to all the other members or parts, great and small. This view of society and sustainable development has three major implications that need to be acknowledged as positive elements:

- Human rights, the rule of law, and the concept of the "common good" are not merely Western values but biological imperatives for sustainability;
- Criteria to use in achieving decentralization, subsidiary governance structures, and their supportive or enabling environments are based on agreed rules. This view replaces plans for streamlining or cost-cutting with changes that are infinitely more far-reaching; it calls for changing or adapting to new processes for policy management and implementation, for public sector housekeeping, and for delivery of public services;
- Closed-system or sectoral approaches to development that are undertaken as discrete activities of fragmented intervention programs are inadequate.

SL policy management must be intersectoral, since it requires interdependent actions from many agencies: public, private, and civic. It must also be interlevel because it requires interdependent actions at all levels of governance. And it must be participatory, consensual, and subsidiary (assigning responsibility at the lowest possible level), because respect for human dignity demands this and it is essential for sustainability. Governments should be concerned with livelihoods on two levels: the household level, where people have the means of supporting themselves; and in society as a whole, where there are the means to provide for the livelihoods of all in the future.

The SL approach, holistic in nature, encourages local people to draw up integrated, multi-sectoral development strategies in order to restore and maintain the health of all aspects of the local social ecosystem. When governance is perceived as the responsibility of all, the distinction between the governing and the governed is progressively blurred. Good governance is self-governance. Society is a living system, and living systems are self-governing. Cells and organisms are each self-governing, though interdependent with the larger organism. And each organism is self-governing and interdependent with the species and the larger ecology. Thus, the aim in developing governance capacity must be to strengthen society's capacity for self-governance at all levels.

The key feature of this system is the self-governance of interdependent individuals, groups, organizations, and institutions, all of which function at different levels of collectivity. Joy explains that this view leads to a new appreciation of the interdependent, synergistic roles of the legislature, the judiciary, the media, the private sector, and civil society in promoting sustainable human development. The design and management of policies and programs, for example, involves issues that are legal, political, economic, and social, and may concern the functions of several agencies, both public and private. Simply assisting separate organizations to become more efficient misses the point.

The need for responsiveness

Societies are sustainable when government is responsive to people's needs and discomforts. Just as environmental sustainability depends upon society's responsiveness to the state of, and trends in, the ecosystem and its ability to correct unsustainable trends, so livelihood sustainability must be approached in the same way. Policy management capacity means, among other things, the daily ability to respond to crises that affect the livelihoods of citizens, whether drought, floods, earthquakes, or changes in international commodity prices. It also means the ability to monitor and respond to warning signals. This implies determining which signals should trigger action, as well as which actions are to be taken and by whom. It also implies financial management that is flexible enough to allow government agencies to spring into action when needed.

When people feel no response to their conditions from society or the state, they become alienated. Crime erupts, "scapegoating" takes hold, and inter- and intracommunity strife escalates. Governance programs, therefore, should aim to improve the responsiveness of public institutions to individuals and group in all parts of society. They should be sensitive to the state of health of society in general and the relationship of each part to the whole. But the onus of response should not be placed solely on government, even though governments do, of course, have responsibility for engagement with the general public.

Capacity development for good governance

While the SL approach does not begin by overanalyzing poverty or needs when working at the community level, governments must, of course, be able to understand the causes of poverty accurately. Thus, analyzes for meeting needs at the local level must address macro policies. Communities need to be encouraged and trained to engage in systemic thinking about their community, its livelihoods systems, and its problems. This should be done in ways that bring home to them their responsibility for their own development. This was demonstrated in Malawi's experience with the Participatory Assessment and Planning for Sustainable Livelihoods (PAPSL) approach, described earlier. Such an approach should involve participation by government, NGOs, civil society organizations and the business community. It should enable those involved to identify the responsibilities of individuals, households, communities, business and civic organizations, and government and international agencies. It should lead to the formation of partnerships for action. Governments should be encouraged to deal with people and communities rather than with numbers, aggregates, and abstractions. Issues of resource allocation should be subordinate to decisions about social action and concern for social relationships.

Policies that support sustainable livelihoods are needed not only in developing countries where poverty is widespread. Countries that are materially affluent are experiencing increasing disruption of livelihoods due to changes in technology, job security, and the nature of employment opportunities.

Improving the processes of decision-making and action should be the goal of international agencies working in the area of governance.

Capacity development for sound governance needs to be explicitly addressed strategically and systemically, which ultimately makes particular demands on leadership. To be effective, such processes must operate competently, with sensitivity and responsiveness to specific, concrete human and environmental concerns. Such processes should reflect fundamental values and principles, such as mutual respect, participation, and even subsidiarity—the practice of assigning responsibility at the lowest possible level.

Capacity development means instituting or strengthening processes and the capacity of organizations to contribute to processes. And it means instituting rules that govern processes. When planning capacity development, one should address several questions:

- Which processes most critically need attention? In other words, what do we most need to attend to in order to restore and maintain the health of our society?
- What needs to be done to design and institutionalize sound processes, rules (formal and informal), and structures? What resources, competencies, and motivations will members of these structures need to play a role in these processes?
- In what order should these tasks be accomplished?
- How should the transition from existing processes to new processes be accomplished?

When building capacity, it is important to set priorities, focusing first on capacities that will have the greatest positive impact on livelihoods. Too vast an agenda can stall the delicate and difficult process of promoting profound cultural change. To ease this process, systems should be made as flexible as possible—ideally, they should be adaptable enough to reinvent themselves when necessary. Their strength should lie in rules and institution rather than in individuals.

In supporting effective processes for good governance, performance criteria should focus specifically on those processes designed to reduce deprivation, economic and social marginalization, and gender inequities, and to promote care for the environment. "Policies should not only help people get out of poverty by strengthening their livelihoods," says Joy. "Policies should reduce vulnerability to shocks and stresses, as well as reducing, so far as possible, the shocks and stresses themselves, or attenuating the trends that produce the shocks and stresses."

Society itself must develop the capacity to understand where it needs to be responsive to external threats and opportunities, and to internal needs, opportunities, and discomforts. The elements that require responses must be made explicit by setting standards in areas such as livelihoods, environmental conditions, gender equity, health care, education, and so on, and by identifying departures from these standards that require response. Processes for maintaining these norms under review are also necessary.

Building social capital, strengthening civil society

The SL approach deals with every facet of the life of people: political, social, cultural, historical. People do not have separate faculties for environment and food security and social interaction. When people participate as citizens, their priorities are defined by how they interact with one another, with the local government, with the central government, with natural stresses and shocks that come to the system, with market forces, and with globalization. All of these affect how people decide on a certain program of action.

When the pressures of shocks and stresses become too great, people lose the incentive to take action. However, important changes occur when the right kind of empowering intervention is applied. Community leaders emerge out of nowhere. People start creating circles and groups. This is called citizen's collective action or social capital, but it requires leadership among the community members themselves. Such developments are the natural effect of involving community members in local development. Projects cannot be designed to create these things. They emerge out of a process in which people engage themselves in development.

An important aspect of capacity development, therefore, is the creation and nurturing of social capital. Another way of describing it is consensually coordinated activities in support of the common good. The task of capacity development is to deepen the organizational structures of society and to encourage flexibility in the processes that allow these structures to relate and interact.

In order to achieve this, capacity development has to take account of the whole governance system, specifically including civil society organizations and the private sector, domestic and foreign. It should seek to maximize complementarity among all actors and in the sequencing of their needed interventions. It should "empower" public institutions, private actors, and civil society organizations by redesigning processes to enable them to work together. The point is to adopt the perspective of systems and systems management in developing strategic policy capacity. "Support for the redesign of policy, planning, and budgeting processes needs to become multi-sectoral and participatory," says Joy.

One effect of the redesigned processes will be to accord new— empowering—roles to civic institutions. This may involve capacity development in existing institutions to enable them to fulfill these roles, the incubation of nongovernmental agencies of all sorts, and the creation of an enabling legal and policy environment in which civil society is nurtured. To do this, it is helpful to ask such questions as:

- How are decisions made and implemented?
- Who plays what role in these processes?
- What values and principles do the decisions reflect?
- What are the constraints faced by each party in fully taking up its new roles and in having its voice heard?
- What needs to be done to relieve these constraints?

The dangers of marginalization

It is useful to pose an even more fundamental question when launching any program of governance and policy capacity development: Why should a government take the trouble to acquire the capacity to manage policies that support sustainable livelihoods? Aside from the moral imperative and economic considerations, there is an answer to this questions that relates directly to the cohesiveness and stability of society itself.

Loss of livelihood is a profound personal affliction and social sickness. When people's livelihoods are jeopardized, threatened, or lost, it is not simply a personal tragedy for those afflicted and a tragic waste of human potential, intelligence, and talents; it becomes a social tragedy because of the alienation and social tension that ensue. Marginalized, displaced, alienated people are symptomatic of social sickness, and this sickness can only be cured by reassimilating them into the economy, society, and polity. Indeed, there are many cases where failure to do so has led to social collapse. The need to focus concern on the problem of marginalization—the displacement of people from the economy, from society, and from political participation—cannot be overemphasized. This problem is not addressed effectively simply by a concern for growth—with or without redistribution—or by increasing employment.

There is also an important link between an indifferent, unresponsive state and overpopulation. "Only by taking care of people and giving them a sense of security will the population explosion be halted," says Joy. "People have large families mainly because it provides the hope that someone will survive to support them in their old age. The dynamic is well understood and documented. It seems not to have registered that the cure for further population explosion is taking care of people, instead of letting Malthusian forces reduce their numbers. This is another important reason why making progress in ensuring sustainable livelihoods should be the highest global priority."

If society is viewed as an organic ecosystem, the alienation or disenfranchisement of any individual or group implies a profound loss to the healthy functioning of the entire system. Conversely, the coming together of those who are marginalized or disenfranchised can confer on them a power and ability to solve problems that nothing else can. Yet in many societies few mechanisms or traditions exist that promote such collective thinking and action on the part of marginalized groups.

Women are a prime example of this phenomenon. "What will empower women," says Sarah Murison, Senior Technical Advisor for Gender and Development at UNDP, "is the opportunity for them to discuss their problems among themselves, define their own solutions, and then be enabled to take action on those solutions." Yet in many cultures there is no tradition for women to do this. Before the PAPSL process took place in the Malawian village of Nyamawende, the community had no tradition of meeting to analyze problems and discuss possible solutions. "Women may need some guidance about how to discuss issues," Murison continues, "especially when doing so is not in their culture."

"There is a new awareness of the need to work from the advocacy of values and principles," says Joy, "notably those of respect, participation, inclusiveness, equity (especially gender equity), subsidiarity, transparency, and accountability, as well as of concern for the well-being of all and for the common good."

Nuts and bolts of good governance

Many steps need to be taken to promote good governance and ensure that national policies support sustainable livelihoods. They may seem overwhelming in their number, intricacy, and scope. Thus, building an "enabling environment" at the national and local levels can be an important beginning to a long and incremental process. Members of the SL International Working Group (IWG) identified a number of levels or "targets of opportunity" where existing processes and institutions may be amenable to change. At the national level these include macro-sectoral policies, bureaucratic mechanisms, financial management, and public administration, as well as initiatives to promote participation and decentralization that are already being launched in many countries. At the local level, processes that support progressive change include initiatives that promote empowerment, participation, and inclusion, as well as those that foster a sense of responsibility among community members.

"The real issue," says Leonard Joy, "is that policy analysis should focus on people and communities, even though the policies that need analysis are all too commonly determined independently by particular (sectoral) ministries. Needed actions are likely to be multi-sectoral. In other words, they will require the engagement of several agencies."

What are some of the tools and methodologies that can be employed to set this mechanism for good governance into motion? At the policy level, the IWG identified a number of tools, ranging from computer simulations of the systems that generate marginalization, to databases, seminars, workshops, consultations, and desk reviews; and from participatory assessments, planning, and implementation, key informants, referenda, and dialogues/consultations, to comparative studies, policy inventories, and gender analysis. In addition, synergies between traditional knowledge and contemporary knowledge need to be promoted, while maintaining the primacy of the people's knowledge, skills, and experience. Among the possible strategies listed were the devolution of decision-making from top to bottom, civic education, gender sensitization, and the advocacy of values, principles, and processes. Structures identified where such strategies can be launched include national, local, and civil society organizations and institutions. Furthermore, the process required to accomplish such changes must be built on consultation, training, awareness, and gender sensitivity. While there was not enough time to elaborate on each of these issues during the course of the workshop, each provides an item for further elaboration and evaluation.

The first step is to redesign the processes and structures and to define how doing so changes existing roles and creates new ones. These role definitions determine what skills are required and what training is needed to produce those skills. A key training method is for participants actually to work on redesigning processes and on identifying new modes of change management and technical cooperation. The style of training programs must be flexible, including explicit training courses and on-the-job orientation and skills modeling.

Screening policies to assess their contribution to sustainable livelihoods involves an analysis of adaptive strategies and continued practices, as well as desk reviews, comparative studies, and inventories of the policies themselves. It requires dialogue both with policy-makers and with those affected by the policies. It should also include gender-sensitive analysis of policies and their effects.

Since good governance is crucial to poverty eradication, the Sustainable Livelihoods approach needs to be applied at all levels—community, regional or district, and national. Achieving good governance means cultivating a coherent public demand for it. Joy points out that the focus on the process of building good governance further underscores the need for "participation and ownership by all participants." However, he also notes that "grassroots self-help activity needs to be integral with systemic strategies to address trends in marginalization and macro policy reviews. Livelihoods issues cannot be effectively tackled at the grassroots level alone."

One of the themes of the SL approach is the linkage, interdependence, or synergy between the micro and the macro, and the important benefits for development that this synergy can produce. For example, added value is achieved when contemporary knowledge is applied to enhance traditional expertise. A linking of "downstream" livelihood programs with "upstream" programs to develop capacity for livelihood policy management should provide for mutually reinforcing efforts. Both are essential, and one without the other will prove ineffective.

In addition to good and bad policies, there are also policies that may have been well intended, but whose impact on livelihoods has proved over time to be harmful rather than supportive. In Zimbabwe, for example, the policy of distributing subsidized maize to villagers in Mlambaphele in times of drought has had the effect of turning people away from the traditional "small grains" of millet and sorghum and given them a taste for maize instead. The problem is that maize cannot be grown in their area because of very low rainfall, whereas small grains can. The latter are far more drought-tolerant. They are also more nutritious than maize, because they can be eaten without a lot of the processing that removes much of the nutritional value of maize. Identifying such "perverse subsidies" and lobbying to change them is the final (though by no means sequentially the last) step of the SL process.

Case study

The Participatory Assessment and Planning process used in Malawi under the SL program fostered ownership at the grassroots level and provided the added value of the development of human capital that is necessary if citizens are to participate meaningfully in self-empowered action. Such a process creates an enabling environment for people to participate and empowers them to take control of their own development and to build their capacity to do so.

At the district level in Malawi, UNDP's Fifth Country Programme provided for capacity building of district-level institutions in six pilot districts, of which Mchinji was one. The goal, according to the program documents, was "to plan and manage development with the active and effective participation of local people." It has become clear that more training in this area is needed, and more training is being organized.

At the government level, UNDP and UNCDF launched a Local Governance and Development Management Programme in partnership with the government of Malawi in 1997. The program document explicitly sees decentralization—increased participation of local people in governance—as a strategy not only for the consolidation of democracy but for poverty alleviation as well. The program aimed "to enhance the capacity for governance and development management of central, district and community level institutions. . . . As part of the process of democracy consolidation and as a strategy for poverty alleviation, the government is pursuing decentralization." Hence in Malawi and throughout the world, if poverty is to be alleviated, indeed eradicated, and if livelihoods are to be made more productive and more sustainable, it is local people who must do the job, aided by the norms and institution of good governance.

Elements of Malawi's Governance and Development Management Programme:
- Creating an enabling environment for public policy and management
- Local governance and development management
- Democracy consolidation
- Gender equality

The program document specifically links poverty with gender inequality. It implies that the establishment of gender equality is not only a necessary end in itself, but also an essential means of eradicating poverty. The document says that unless discrimination against women and girls at all levels is ended, and unless women are empowered and given equal rights to land, credit, and jobs, and unless action is taken to end violence against women, overall poverty eradication cannot take place.

A number of steps are planned to increase the role of women in decision-making. Gender analysis, training, and awareness programs are being organized at the central and district levels. Gender issues and women's participation will be a focal point of institutional strengthening and capacity building activities. For all training events, a goal of 25 percent female participants has been set. One elected woman and one man from each Village Development Committee will serve on every Area Development Committee, and 35 percent of the members of all training teams will be women.

Additional donor initiatives for the promotion of participatory democracy and human rights include the Democracy Project of GTZ (the German aid agency). This agency supports civic education for local government elections; initiatives for strengthening the institutional capacity of electoral commissions in order to effectively manage national and local elections, funded by USAID; and capacity building programs in support of decentralization policy implementation, funded by GTZ and Danida, the aid agency of Denmark.

It is also interesting that of the four impact areas targeted by the program, those of most intense focus are local and regional, building governance from the "bottom up." Not only is capacity building planned for a wide range of institutions engaged in decentralization and local governance, but the most basic needs of local people for investments, infrastructures, and services are also to be addressed, in order to foster an enabling environment for local empowerment. District Development Funds are to be greatly expanded as the primary conduit for financing district-level development throughout the country. Infrastructure and services are to be expanded and improved, particularly in the rural areas, and people will be made aware of the potential role of local government in improving living conditions and broadening their participation in decision-making. Various courses, workshops, and follow-up visits on decentralization policy are planned for groups ranging from officials of the central government to members of District Development Committees, Area Development Committees, and Village Development Committees.

Environmental concerns will be incorporated into all development initiatives from their inception. To do this, guidelines for the assessment of environmental impacts have been prepared and will be followed by the District Executive Committees as they design, appraise, and implement proposed projects. Capacity building activities will also seek to support and reinforce improved management of natural resources at all levels.

In Malawi, where colonialism was followed by dictatorship, people tend to be cynical about government. Paradoxically, while viewing central authority as a threat and an oppressor, they also tend to look to government to solve all their problems. Donor relations also often create a sense of dependency on the part of communities, local authorities, and even the government itself. Passivity, fatalism, and inertia at all levels can be the result. However, attitudes are beginning gradually to change. Dominico Nkhuwa, the son of the chief in Nyamawende, has grasped the shift in thinking that must take place. "With the change of our government to democracy, we should not misunderstand the concept," he says. "Democracy does not mean we should be sitting idle. It means we should be independent and self-reliant."

The passage from a centralized, authoritarian state to a decentralized democracy is a tortuous journey and cannot be achieved overnight. In Malawi, culture and history tend to reinforce the status quo. "People are used to being told what to do," says Kristine Jones, PAPSL advisor to the National Economic Council of Malawi. "In the past, the central government thought up good policies or bad polices and imposed them. What the SL program is trying to do is turn that around so that policy is informed by people on the ground, by rural communities,"

An analysis is already under way within the context of Malawi's food security program to determine the impact of existing policies on food security. Bunda College of Agriculture has prepared a policy review, and areas that need attention have been identified. After editing, the review will be presented to the government for discussion of policy changes that need to be made. But Malawi still has a long way to go in drafting policies that systematically make sustainable livelihoods a priority. In the policy arena the old practice of dividing development into sectors is still in place. "As of now we do not have a 'Sustainable Livelihoods policy.'" says Peter Kulemeka. "What we have are policies for specific sectors, for example, food security. We have also have policies in a draft form on microenterprise development, and we have policies relating to the environment, all of which target the sort of people who are also the target group of the Sustainable Livelihoods program. We are hopeful that in the future there will be changes in support of the Sustainable Livelihoods approach."

In the longer term, a central idea of the SL approach is that the process of democratization taking place in Malawi, and in many countries throughout the world, will increasingly enable local people and the organizations that represent them to serve as "watchdogs" over policies at the macro level that affect livelihoods at the micro level. Such grassroots advocates will increasingly be able to "lobby" policymakers to design policies aimed at making livelihoods more sustainable and more productive, rather than the reverse.

One way of doing this is through civic education, and the courses and workshops planned in Malawi will probably be just the beginning of a long process. Civic education can serve as a building block with other SL activities designed to produce the outcome of sustainable livelihoods. If civic education leads to an improved awareness in people of how they relate to other members of the community—to society, to local government, and to the state—then that reflects synergy with economic efficiency and environmental resilience. It brings in the element of social equity. People are aware of their rights and privileges and their entitlements. These are the building blocks of sustainable livelihoods. This kind of synergy evolves organically in the long term.

Nevertheless, by including SL priorities from the outset—economic efficiency, ecological integrity, and society equity—the building blocks of sustainable development will be in place and will not need to be added and coordinated at a later date. "We are using the tools of strategic planning and management for administration coordination," says B. T. Costantinos, team leader of the SL program in Malawi, "and we are using multi-track communications to ensure that there is a smooth flow of information among the different activities that are being implemented. So already, the synergy is being created while the building blocks are in progress. Sustainable livelihoods are an organic output of this synergy."

One of the essential aspects of good governance is communication: a free press, access to information, and channels through which people at all levels can communicate with one another. UNDP's resident representative in Malawi, Terence Jones, points out that the entire SL program has been designed to promote the responsiveness of government to the people. "We are trying to devolve government responsibilities to the district level so that government is close to the people and more responsive, and responsible, to the people," says Jones. "This approach, from what we have seen so far, generates effective demand from the communities and empowers them to access resources available from government and NGOs and others. It's a nice combination of trying to make government closer to the people from the top, and building the demand from the bottom, and hoping the two will work effectively together."

Such effectiveness will depend to a large extend on effective communications, and the SL program is also working to set up multi-track communications systems that identify a variety of ways in which the various actors in development can communicate most successfully with each other. "We are exploring the various types of media that will be most effective in communicating between any two groups," says Jones. "It could be policy-makers and villagers, villagers and extension agents, donors and policy-makers, donors and villagers." For example, UNESCO is supporting an experiment with community radio to enable communities to produce useful programming for communicating among themselves about issues and problems. In another program, plays and musical productions are being successfully used to convey messages. And in another district, plans are in the works to train journalists based in rural areas to interview community members in order to produce programs that can be aired on the radio for discussion with policy-makers. "It is like a feedback mechanism," says Jones.

Another essential element of good governance is the often overlooked truth that government institutions exist to serve the needs of the people. While even those who apply the SL approach may sometimes forget this, the approach itself can be a powerful tool for linking government-level expertise with the people who most need such support. "We have not done everything perfectly from the beginning," concedes Lalao Ramanarivo, assistant resident representative of UNDP in Madagascar. "For example, we did not call upon the technical services of the various ministries when we began our SL program. However, after we looked at the results of our community assessments, we did involve them. The ministries said they could help the peasants improve their techniques of coffee growing. We said, better late than never. Since then we have been involving the ministries from the beginning of the process. Now, as we are starting the second phase, we are going to make sure that government institutions are involved from the beginning, so we will see the various roles each ministry can play, whether in the area of technology or environmental management or whatever. We are trying to promote a participatory approach."

This raises another crucial issue. "When ministries have overall national budgets and nationally designed programs, the expenditure allocation to the various districts is not generally readily flexible," says Leonard Joy. "What is required is budgeting that starts by determining and mediating the claims of the districts and then adding these up so that the overall budget of the ministry is the sum of district needs plus the amount needed to provide central services. This also changes the character of ministries, enabling them to operate more like consulting and technical assistance agencies, and less like the implementers of government-imposed programs."

―――― TIPS AND LESSONS LEARNED ――――

◆ Inclusiveness, decentralization, and consensus characterize good governance. It is non-coercive, responsible, ethical, judicious, credible, accountable, and transparent.

◆ Norms, standards or models of good governance must be defined.

◆ Commitments to promote good governance must be secured from those in power.

◆ Departures from the norms of good governance must be carefully monitored.

◆ A systemic understanding of what good governance is and how it works must be cultivated and translated into strategies, programs, and budgets.

♦ Mechanisms to generate feedback from the grassroots level to government circles must be put in place, as well as mechanisms that foster accountability on the part of government institutions.

♦ The ability to make decisions at the local level must be greatly enhanced.

♦ A policy analysis that links macro causes to micro effects needs to be carried out to identify which policies, or combinations of policies, disrupt adaptive strategies or livelihood systems, and which policies reinforce such strategies and systems.

Epilogue

In introducing the Sustainable Livelihoods approach in some detail, this book has attempted to redefine development in terms of what human beings need most, and especially in terms of what they already have. It has sought to direct the focus of development thinking toward supporting the talents, the knowledge, and the expertise of individual human beings. Understanding people and their local context, and helping to create the enabling environment in which they can use their abilities, fulfill their potential, and flourish—this should be the aim of development.

We are not just interested in survival or in fulfilling basic needs. There should be no limits to what people can achieve, to their ability to solve problems and prosper, and to the quality of life they can attain. The human rights theme is due for a revival. The right in question is more than the right not to be marginalized, it is the right to pursue a livelihood. People tend to consider human rights as a means to protect themselves, whereas human rights should also be understood as responsibilities that we have toward others; not simply protecting the rights of others, but recognizing that their dignity has to be preserved by us, by society as a whole. If society is an ecosystem, the right to a sustainable livelihood, and the dignity this right confers on everyone, is essential to society's survival and is the collective responsibility of all strata of society. Conversely, while society is responsible for upholding the rights and dignity of the individual, the individual is also responsible to society.

If the right to a sustainable livelihood is a basic human right that is being recognized more and more around the world, upholding this right is the business of international agencies and development NGOs as they work to eradicate poverty and build capacity for good governance.

Sustainable Livelihoods at a Glance

The basic premise: Livelihoods

The essential element at the root of all human development and economic growth is livelihoods. This means much more than jobs. It covers the wide, infinitely diverse range of things people do to make their living. Understanding what livelihoods consist of and how they work is therefore the best guide to understanding how livelihoods can be made more productive and more sustainable.

Livelihoods consist of:

- **activities**, such as work, in the formal and informal sectors
- **assets**, which can be divided into four categories:
  - human capital
    - skills
    - knowledge
    - creativity
    - adaptive strategies
  - social capital
    - governance structures
    - decision-making power
    - community and other institutions
    - culture
    - participatory processes
  - natural capital
    - land
    - water
    - air
    - forestry/vegetation

      – human-made capital
        buildings
        roads
        machinery
        crops/livestock
- **entitlements**
  - the support of family or clan members
  - rights enshrined in national constitutions and international treaties
  - technical assistance from extension workers
  - in industrialized countries, social security and unemployment insurance
- **short-term coping mechanisms** in response to shocks and stresses
- **adaptive strategies**, the long-term changes and adjustments people make in their livelihood systems in order to respond to difficult circumstances. Adaptive strategies serve as the entry point of the SL approach.

Sustainability

Sustainability is a key indicator of success. Projects that are based on empowerment and improvements in the livelihoods of the poor stand a much better chance of surviving than projects that fade away with the depletion of initial funding and efforts.

The SL approach has the potential for ensuring sustainability because it tends to go deeper into livelihood systems and to examine such areas as natural resource endowment and the relationship of communities to policy and local governance. This provides a better chance of understanding some of the conditions that have to be met if efforts are to be sustained over time.

To be sustainable, a livelihood system must:

- be **economically efficient**, rather than wasteful, in its use of resources.
- adhere to the precepts of **social equity**, that is, the way one household or community makes its livelihood must not disrupt options for others to make their livelihood. Indeed, whenever possible, one form of livelihood should enhance other livelihoods, as happens in relationships of trade, exchange, and services.

- obey the laws of **ecological integrity**, preserving or restoring resources for use by future generations.
- be **resilient**, able to cope with, and recover from, shocks and stresses.

Sustainable Livelihoods and gender

It is important to acknowledge openly and take into account the distinctive roles of women and the special obstacles they face. An analysis of the adaptive strategies of women may often be different from an analysis of the adaptive strategies of men.

Promoting Sustainable Livelihoods

Development is a multifaceted process that must be approached in a holistic, integrated manner. The SL approach uses the well-known building blocks of development—income-generation, environmental management, women's empowerment, education, health care, appropriate technology, financial services, and good governance—to create a synergy that produces sustainable livelihoods. SL combines a number of approaches, using elements of each. However, none of these approaches can individually produce the same effect, the same level of genuine participatory empowerment, that the SL approach can achieve.

Promoting SL involves determining what the people already know. Support for existing livelihoods systems ensures sustainability and seeks to increase productivity.

The interactive participatory components are:

- Understanding adaptive strategies
- Analysis of current policies and governance issues that impinge on people's livelihood strategies
- Identification of appropriate technology, which improves productivity
- Identification of social and economic investment mechanisms that help existing livelihoods strategies by improving, producing, or creating new opportunities
- Development of SL indicators to monitor the progress of different programs

A basic tenet of the SL approach is that adaptive strategies can be made more productive and more sustainable with the application of:

- contemporary knowledge or technology
- financial services, such as credit and savings
- improvements in government policies

The SL approach is not a fixed template or formula. Rather, it is an intellectual reminder of the multidimensionality of community life, and of the need to cover all the bases of this multidimensionality. Therein lies the promise of sustainability.

The Process

Traditionally, the concept of development has been defined in terms of infrastructure. However, development should focus on people, their attitudes and practices. After individuals are empowered, they take responsibility for their own development, including looking after the infrastructural matters that complement the changes that have taken place within the individual. Every aspect of the SL approach is based on the empowerment of the people so that they can take charge of their own development.

> The simple act of focusing on what people already have, what they already know and do—instead of on what they need—shifts the perception the poor have of themselves from one of helpless victims of circumstance to one of capable actors who can control their own destiny.

A key element that sets SL apart from traditional approaches to development is that it deliberately and systematically seeks to avoid creating a donor-recipient syndrome among the poor. Researchers present themselves to a village as respectful learners seeking a better understanding of development from the people's point of view.

SL facilitators focus on a community's assets, strategies, and strengths rather than on its needs. As a result, a sense of equality develops between villagers and development workers, and villagers do not feel inferior.

From the very beginning the SL approach sets out to shatter stereotypes about the "superior" knowledge of educated outsiders as compared to that of "ignorant" villagers.

Training for facilitators

Members of the educated elite, even if they are engaged in development work, tend carefully to maintain a personal distance and sense of superiority in all their interactions with the poor. This is a phenomenon that can be a serious obstacle to the empowerment of the poor. Development workers need to be carefully cultivated by assiduous attitudinal training so that villagers can start the process of community consciousness-raising needed to reshape their expectations of development workers and of themselves.

Training for villagers

In many cultures throughout the developing world, the ravages of history have stifled individual initiative, confidence, and self-reliance. The purpose of the training is to help community members look at themselves in order to discover how they have internalized their social and cultural sense of reality, and to start exploring new options.

Participatory research

Several different styles and methods of participatory research exist. For example, Participatory Rural appraisal (PRA) practitioners assume roles of respectful outsiders who work to legitimize local knowledge and promote community empowerment. The Participatory Assessment and Planning for Sustainable Livelihoods (PAPSL) guidebook is an effective tool that builds on the various styles of participatory research and guides facilitators seeking to empower villagers. PAPSL is a fusion of three development methodologies:

- Training for Transformation, which seeks to "awaken" and "empower" the poor so they will take charge of their own development;
- Participatory Rural Appraisal, a system of research and information-gathering that involves local people in a detailed study of their community and livelihood systems; and
- a planning methodology designed to produce strategies for action.

The PAPSL methodology proposes six steps of project execution:

1. Identify and conceptualize projects and outline the responsibilities of sponsoring international agencies to coordinate the projects
2. Address the principles needed in selecting countries in which to conduct participatory research
3. In-country preparation (formal permission and clearances, etc.)
4. Participatory fieldwork methods and techniques
5. Examine the policies that impinge on local livelihood realities
6. Outline outputs and follow-up

Women are central to development

Women are usually the chief engine of development in a community. They are most often the group that will later implement the Action Plans. The barriers and obstacles that women experience need to be taken into account, since they tend to have a depressing effect on livelihoods at the household level.

Science and technology

In many cases, a first step toward helping to strengthen livelihood systems consists of an application of science or technology that brings improvements in

- agriculture or animal husbandry
- industry
- commerce
- housing
- infrastructure
- communications

as well as providing training in more effective, more productive, more sustainable ways of making a living.

The contemporary knowledge that SL facilitators bring to a community should complement and improve on the strategies and systems the people have already developed.

Sustainable technologies

The primary purpose of sustainable technologies is to create livelihoods—jobs that do not destroy the environment, that are good for women, and that are local and small scale. The second purpose of sustainable technologies is to satisfy basic needs—shelter, water, energy, clothing, paper—that people have no other way to satisfy. If technology is to strengthen sustainable livelihoods,

- it must be "appropriate" to local needs and conditions
- it must create meaningful jobs rather than eliminating them
- it must not disrupt existing livelihoods systems
- it should be labor-saving rather than labor-intensive
- it must preserve, enhance, and enrich the local environment rather than depleting it

Ashok Khosla, director of Development Alternatives in India, expands on these parameters of sustainable technology as follows:

- Sustainable technology is relevant and ready for use by the common people, and aims directly to improve the quality of their lives.
- Sustainable technology derives maximum leverage from the local environment by drawing upon existing managerial and technical skills, and providing the basis for extending them.
- Sustainable technology uses the physical potential of an area and maintains harmony between people and nature.

Methodology

- **National level**—concentrate on the formulation and adoption of technology policies, such as outlining strategic goals or introducing incentives for collaboration between public an private sectors
- **Meso-level**—develop institutional support
- **Local level**—assess the current technology level, needs, and constraints

Phosiso Sola, biologist and SL facilitator in Zimbabwe, says:

Before we started talking about what we might bring in as outsiders, the people realized that they have the means of solving their problems. All they needed is technical expertise: a "jump start" to help them get moving. This makes them "own" the project. It also means that the project will be sustainable, that it will continue after the agency has pulled out.

Not only is there an obvious need for a vast array of simple technologies, but there is no lack of designs for them as well. The constraints to producing them on a large scale, however, are many. Considerations include:

- capital and operational costs
- efficiency of the technology
- ease of operation and ergonomic design
- availability of spare parts
- ease of repair and maintenance
- problems of production
- adaptation to local conditions
- existence of marketing organizations
- promotion, training, extension services,
- management skills

Widespread dissemination of sustainable technologies requires important changes in the way industries work, such as:

- new types of institutional structures to carry out new kinds of functions
- the decentralization of innovation, production, and marketing to respond to local needs and conditions
- a large enough product range and territorial coverage to provide economies of scale in innovation, manufacturing, and marketing
- the development of clusters and packages of technologies to take advantage of standardized modules and components for facilitating production, marketing, spare-parts availability, and maintenance.

Sharing information

As part of the Malawian government's SL program, a multi-track communications system is being set up. It will describe examples of technology that have been successfully applied in the local context, with simple instructions on how such technologies can be implemented. The system will be used for accessing information about new technologies and for learning about experiences with technology in other districts.

Other examples of technology networks (also see Resources herein):

- Paul Harrison's 1987 book, *The Greening of Africa*, describes many simple technologies and applications of scientific knowledge that are being applied more and more to improve environmental conditions and increase agricultural productivity in many parts of Africa.
- Development Alternatives (DA) has established a network that provides access to information on sustainable development. It can connect users to the many databases of ENVIS, India's Ministry of Environment and Forests Department of Science and Technology.
- A large network set up by SRISTI (Society for Research and Initiatives for Sustainable Technologies and Institutions) reaches seventy-five countries. The SRISTI-Honey Bee network of grassroots innovators and inventions lists, among other things, local institutions involved in natural resource management that are initiated and governed by local people. The SRISTI-Honey Bee network newsletter is published in English and five Indian languages, as well as in Zonkha, the language of Bhutan.

Investments and financial services

Building blocks and synergy

The American Heritage Dictionary defines *synergy* as the interaction of two or more agents or forces so that their combined effect is greater than the sum of their individual effects. The building blocks that produce the synergy of elements that lead to sustainable livelihoods are well-known development techniques:

- Participation and empowerment foster self-confidence and initiative.
- Access to science and appropriate technology promotes economic efficiency and ecological integrity.
- Investments and financial services promote resilience and nurture economic efficiency.

- Good governance and policies set the stage for social equity, which in turn strengthens the sustainable interplay of all the other elements.

When enterprises are launched or credit is initially extended in keeping with social equity and ecological integrity, the outcome is much more likely to be livelihood systems that are sustainable, that is, equitable, efficient, environmentally benign, and resilient.

B. T. Costantinos, team leader of UNDP's SL Programme, Malawi, says:

> Once you have economic growth going in its own direction, then to correct the damage caused to the environment, you'll need another project in environmental rehabilitation. So instead, you design your economic development and growth programs in such a way that they are environmentally sustainable from the beginning. That's the kind of synergy I'm talking about.

And Ashok Khosla comments,

> Credit is very important, but you've also got to introduce technologies, increase productivity, and improve the ability of people to generate and save money, and invest it for further improvements in productivity.

What is needed is the micro-macro linkage that expands income-generating activities through the marriage of "outside" to "inside" technology, enabling the poor to move beyond the subsistence level to greater productivity while maintaining environmental sustainability.

The complex issue of credit for women

Increased access to capital has been linked by studies to greater political participation and bargaining power for women in the home, and to greater expenditures on food, health, and education. However, credit does not necessarily mean empowerment. As Sarah Murison, UNDP's Senior Technical Advisor for Gender and Development, points out:

> Attempts to deliver microfinance and at the same time to give women opportunities to meet together and discuss

issues that would empower them have been found not to be going on. It requires very different skills to be a loan officer and to be a community development worker. The assumption that combining microfinance with empowering activities is possible seems to be incorrect.

Ironically, the high rates at which women repay their loans may be a function of their low status—of their disempowerment.

Whether doing better financially confers a degree of empowerment on women or not is unresolved. The key question—also unclear—is whether microfinance does in fact lead to increases in income. Sometimes it does, but not always. Murison continues:

> It is well known that the money often goes straight into the hands of men, and they use it for their businesses. Very often the women are sent by their husbands to get the loans. This would not necessarily be a bad thing if the family income were equally shared within the household.

It has been documented in many countries that men tend to spend their income on their own amusements rather than on their families.

Key points on the issue of credit for women:

- Credit does not necessarily lead to improved income.
- If there is improved income, this probably does improve the status of women. However, it may not necessarily do so when their low status derives from factors other than income.
- The method of delivery of the finance may be inherently disempowering, because getting high rates of return is not automatic. It often involves putting pressure on women.
- Credit can only pay for empowerment if there is a distinct linear relationship among credit, improved income, and improved status. Such a relationship has not yet been fully demonstrated.
- It may be possible to demonstrate a correlation between extremely low status and high repayment rates.

Flexibility, expansion, and diversification

Without flexibility, microfinance programs can become increasingly supply-driven and institutionally focused, tending to adhere to the goals and agenda of donor institutions, rather than being driven by demand, responsive to clients' needs and supportive of clients' strengths.

An emphasis on growth-oriented investments at the expense of other factors often bypasses the most vulnerable populations and may indirectly disadvantage women.

Microfinance programs must be guided by, and tailored to, the needs and the proven adaptive strategies of the poor themselves, both as a starting point and as a means of evaluating success.

Investment strategies must be designed in such a way that they strengthen each phase of the employment-generation cycle, including promotion, production, and marketing.

Investment strategies should also emphasize the development of sustainable local financial institutions responsive to local needs.

Proponents of SL point out the need for a menu of approaches flexible enough to support all types of financial strategies, particularly those that may fall through the cracks of more standardized schemes. The question is not which investment strategy is the "best practice," but which is best for supporting certain livelihood systems in a particular context at a particular time.

Poor people, particularly women, often become adept at judging local markets and the potential viability of various income-generating activities, for without such astuteness they could not survive.

To promote sustainable livelihoods, a broader conceptual framework for investments is needed:

- emergency resources
- expanded skills training
- appropriate technology
- the nurturing of environmental resources

At the national level, high priority should be placed on investments that support livelihoods, such as:

- social investments in non-formal and formal education
- health
- emergency aid and relief
- political participation
- sound local governance
- community-based programs that restore and preserve the environment

The SL approach to investments demands the same diversity and flexibility as is found in the actual livelihood systems and adaptive strategies of the people themselves. Moreover, financial services should promote ongoing diversification and flexibility in people's livelihood systems, enabling them constantly to adapt, expand, and respond to new circumstances.

To more appropriately meet the specific needs of a wide range of individuals living in diverse situations, investment strategies can be thought of as belonging to one of three categories:

- survival strategies
- stability strategies
- accumulation strategies

Survival strategies

People in marginal situations, such as those living in fragile ecosystems, post-conflict or resettlement areas, remote rural areas and urban squatter settlements, need risk-reduction strategies with a heavy emphasis on social investments such as health care and education. The public sector and/or donor agencies should target investments toward supporting the people's traditional coping mechanisms, as well as health, education, social mobilization, and the strengthening of civil society organizations.

Stability strategies

Poor households and communities are often involved in subsistence, small-holder agriculture, street-vending, petty trade, or commerce. Investment schemes for these clients should include:

- stabilizing mechanisms such as precautionary savings programs
- access to working capital
- consumption credit
- insurance schemes

Collateral should be flexible and non-exclusionary. Such an approach is needed to smooth consumption, increase the capacity to bear risk, and enable the poor to invest in assets for long-term security.

Accumulation strategies

Accumulation strategies emphasize growth or expansion through small-scale agriculture, small and medium enterprises, and small industrial activities. For these clients, savings schemes are important as insurance against hard times, but more emphasis should be placed on technological support, vocational training, and education.

Governance and policy

Sound governance is central to sustainable human development, economic viability, and poverty eradication. Policy and governance are key elements required to promote the economic efficiency, ecological integrity, and social equity that make up sustainable livelihoods. As Ashok Khosla says:

> Perhaps the most important prerequisite for creating sustainable livelihoods, and indeed for achieving sustainable development, is good and accessible government.

Thierry Lemaresquier, director of UNDP's Social Development and Poverty Elimination Division, believes:

> Removing those policies that are obstacles to true development is the key. Using the sustainable livelihoods approach to do this can be quite effective.

The greatest challenge to attaining sustainable livelihoods lies in the weaknesses of many third world governments, particularly in Africa. Such lack of sound governance is typically characterized by:

- stagnant, inept, and unresponsive bureaucracies
- inconsistent administrative machineries
- corrupt institutions
- a lack of transparency in fiscal affairs
- a lack of commitment to upholding the constitution or bill of rights, where these exist, or reluctance to formulate such norms and standards where they do not exist

What characterizes the type of governance that supports sustainable livelihoods?

- At the national level it must be credible and predictable.
- Its macro policies must be informed by micro realities and characterized by fiscal prudence.
- Its policies must be pro-poor.
- Its policies must empower and benefit the poor and, wherever possible, be generated through the participation of the poor themselves.
- At the local level such policies must be informed by gender- and power-sensitivity.
- Its policies must be designed to improve the livelihoods of the poor.

Many governments need help in building systems, policies, and processes that promote and support sustainable livelihoods. One way to do this is to encourage a shift from the compartmentalized, sectoral approach to development to a more integrated, multi-stakeholder, and holistic approach that creates a synergy among the economic, ecological and social dimensions of sustainable development.

Monitoring unemployment is not the same as asking if people are able to provide for themselves. A livelihood is not an optional extra. It is the very basis of survival, of society and of economic stability. Unless the causes of disrupted livelihoods are addressed, attempts to secure sustainable livelihoods will be fragmented and will not eradicate poverty in any meaningful way or on a large scale.

Leonard Joy, a UNDP consultant, puts it this way:

> The goal of supporting sustainable livelihoods through policy management is to ensure that there is productive, fulfilling, healthy, non-exploitative, non-coercive, non-dependent, environmentally sustainable work that provides for all to be self-supporting at an acceptable material level of living, and for all to be fully assimilated into the economy and society.

Society as ecosystem

A number of development thinkers today find it useful to regard society as an ecosystem, a living organism in which each part or member has a crucial role to play that helps sustain the whole, and in which each lives in an interdependent relationship with all the other members or parts, great and small.

This view of society and sustainable development presents human rights, the rule of law, and the concept of the "common good" not merely as Western values but as biological imperatives for sustainability. It replaces plans for streamlining or cost-cutting with changes that are infinitely more far-reaching: the adaptation to new processes for policy management and implementation, public-sector housekeeping, and the delivery of public services. Leonard Joy says that:

> Processes of livelihood policy management must be:
> * intersectoral, since they require interdependent actions from many agencies, public, private and civic;
> * interlevel because they require interdependent actions at all levels of governance;
> * participatory, consensual, and subsidiary (assigning responsibility at the lowest possible level), because respect for human dignity demands this, and it is essential for sustainability.

Sound governance is self-governance

As governance is seen as the responsibility of all, the distinction between the governing and the governed is progressively blurred. Thus the aim of governance capacity development must be to strengthen society's capacity for self-governance at all levels. Joy says:

> There is a new view of governance in which the government is only part of a national governance system. Good governance is self-governance. Society is a living system and living systems are self-governing. Cells and organisms are each self-governing, though interdependent with the larger organism. And each organism is self-governing and interdependent with the species and the larger ecology.

This view leads to a new appreciation of the interdependent, synergistic roles of the legislature, the judiciary, the media, the private sector, and civil society in promoting sustainable human development.

When it comes to the design and management of policies and programs, legal, political, economic, and social contexts often need to be addressed, and several agencies, public and private, may need to be involved. Simply assisting separate organizations to become more efficient misses the point.

Capacity development for good governance

The goal of international agencies working in the area of governance should be to improve the processes of decision-making and action. To be effective, such processes must operate competently, with sensitivity and responsiveness to specific, concrete human and environmental concerns. "The process of capacity development for sound governance needs to be explicitly addressed strategically and systemically," says Joy.

Capacity development is about processes. It means instituting or strengthening processes and organizations' capacities to contribute to processes, and it means instituting rules that govern processes. When planning capacity development, it is important to define

- which processes most critically need attention; that is, what is needed in order to restore and maintain the health of our society;
- what needs to be done with regard to the design and institutionalization of sound processes, rules (formal and informal), and structures, including their resources, competencies, and the motivations of their members to play a role in these processes;
- in what order these tasks should be accomplished;
- how the transition from existing processes to new processes should be accomplished.

When building capacity, it is important to set priorities, focusing first on capacities that will have the greatest positive impact on livelihoods.

Systems should be made as flexible as possible—ideally they should be adaptable enough to reinvent themselves when necessary. Their strength should lie in rules and institutions rather than in individuals.

In supporting effective processes for good governance, performance criteria should focus specifically on those processes designed to reduce deprivation, economic and social marginalization, and gender inequities, and to promote care for the environment.

Leonard Joy says:

> Policies should not only help people get out of poverty by strengthening their livelihoods. Policies should reduce vulnerability to shocks and stresses, as well as reducing, so far as possible, the shocks and stresses themselves, or attenuating the trends that produce the shocks and stresses.

Analysis for meeting needs at the local level must address macro policies needed to counter the most pervasive and deep-rooted trends. Communities need to be encouraged—indeed, trained—to engage in systemic thinking about their community—its livelihoods systems and its problems—in ways that bring home to them their responsibility for their own development.

Governments should be encouraged to deal with people and communities, rather than with numbers, aggregates and abstractions.

The need for responsiveness

Societies are sustainable when government is responsive to people's needs and discomforts. When people feel no response to their condition from society or the state, they become alienated. Crime erupts, scapegoating takes hold and inter- and intracommunity strife escalates.

Policy management capacity means, among other things, the day-to-day ability to respond to crises that affect the livelihoods of citizens—whether droughts, floods, earthquakes, or changes in international commodity prices. It also means the ability to monitor, and respond to, warning signals.

Governance programs should aim to improve the responsiveness of public institutions to individuals and groups in all parts of society, including sensitivity to the state of health of society in general and the relationship of each part to the whole.

Society itself must develop the capacity to understand where it needs to be responsive to external threats and opportunities and to internal needs, opportunities and discomforts. This responsiveness requires explicit attention to setting standards in areas such as:

- livelihoods
- environmental conditions
- gender equity
- health care
- education

Building social capital, strengthening civil society

An important aspect of capacity development is the creation and nurturing of social capital, or consensually coordinated activities in support of the common good.

When the pressures of shocks and stresses become too great, people lose the incentive to take action. They become fatalistic. But when the right kind of empowering intervention is applied, important changes occur. B. T. Costantinos puts it this way:

> When there is somebody to encourage them, to explain that there are ways and means in which other societies have made it out of similar poverty, then people get motivated. Then you get community leaders who emerge out of nothing. People start creating circles and groups. This is what we call citizen's collective action or social capital, but it needs leadership among the community members themselves. You cannot design a project to create these things. They emerge out of a process in which people engage themselves in development.

Societal development implies a deepening of the organizational structures of society and a flexibility in the processes that allow these structures to relate and interact. This is the task of capacity development.

Governance capacity development should take account of the whole governance system—including civil society organizations and the private sector, domestic and foreign—and of the importance of complementarity and sequence of needed interventions.

Capacity development for strategic policy management needs to be seen from the perspective of systems and systems management, in which *empowerment* means redesigning processes so that public institutions, private actors, and civil society organizations can work in partnership with one another.

New processes will accord new—empowering—roles to civic institutions, which may require capacity development to enable them to fulfill these roles. This may involve developing the capacities of existing institutions, as well as the incubation of non governmental agencies of all sorts.

The creation of an enabling legal and policy environment in which civil society is nurtured may be required. To do this, it is helpful to ask:

- How are decisions made and implemented?
- Who plays what role in these processes?
- What values and principles do they reflect?
- What are the constraints faced by each party in fully taking up its new roles and in having its voice heard?
- What needs to be done to relieve these constraints?

The dangers of marginalization

Why should a government take the trouble to acquire the capacity to manage policies that support sustainable livelihoods? There is an answer to this question that relates directly to the cohesiveness and stability of society itself; that is, "loss of livelihood is a profound personal affliction and social sickness," as Leonard Joy says. When people's livelihoods are jeopardized, threatened, or lost, it is not simply a personal tragedy for those afflicted and a tragic waste of human potential, intelligence, and talents. It becomes a social tragedy because of the alienation and social tension that ensue.

Marginalized, displaced, alienated people are symptomatic of social sickness, and this sickness can be cured only by reassimilating them into the economy, society, and polity. Indeed, there are many cases where failure to do so has led to social collapse.

We cannot overemphasize the need to focus concern on the problem of marginalization—the displacement of people from the economy, from society, and from political participation. This problem is not addressed effectively simply by a concern for growth—with or without redistribution—or by increasing employment.

Leonard Joy continues:

> Only by taking care of people and giving them a sense of security will the population explosion be halted. People have large families mainly because this provides the hope that someone will survive to support them in their old age. The dynamic is well understood and documented. It seems not to have registered that the cure for further population explosion is taking care of people instead of letting Malthusian forces reduce their numbers. This is another important reason why making progress in ensuring sustainable livelihoods should be of the highest global priority.

If society is viewed as an organic ecosystem, the alienation or disenfranchisement of any individual or group implies a profound loss to the healthy functioning of the entire system. Conversely, the coming together of those who are marginalized or disenfranchised can confer on them a power and ability to solve problems that nothing else can.

"What will empower women is the opportunity for them to discuss their problems among themselves, define their own solutions, and then be enabled to take action on those solutions," says Murison. "Women may need some guidance about how to discuss issues, especially when doing so is not in the culture."

Leonard Joy adds:

> There is a new awareness of the need to work from the advocacy of values and principles, notably those of respect, participation, inclusiveness, equity (especially gender equity), subsidiarity, transparency, and accountability, and of concern for the well-being of all and for the common good.

Nuts and bolts of good governance

Good governance is characterized by:

- inclusiveness
- decentralization
- consensus

It is non-coercive, responsible, ethical, judicious, credible, accountable, and transparent.

Building an "enabling environment" at the national and local levels can be an important beginning to the long and incremental process of promoting good governance.

A number of levels or "targets of opportunity" have been identified where existing processes and institutions may be amenable to change. At the national level these include:

- macro sectorial policies
- bureaucratic mechanisms
- financial management
- public administration
- initiatives to promote participation and decentralization

At the local level, processes that support progressive change include initiatives that

- promote empowerment, participation and inclusion; and
- foster a sense of responsibility among community members.

A number of capacities are needed to identify needed changes in policies and to put new policies in place. For example:

- Norms, standards, or models of good governance must be defined.
- Commitments to promote good governance must be secured from those in power.
- Departures from the norms of good governance must be carefully monitored.
- A systemic understanding of what good governance is and how it works must be cultivated and translated into strategies, programs, and budgets.
- Mechanisms to generate feedback from the grassroots level to government circles must be put in place.
- Mechanisms that foster accountability on the part of government institutions must be established.
- The ability to make decisions at the local level must be greatly enhanced.
- A policy analysis that links macro causes to micro effects needs to be carried out to identify which policies or combinations of policies disrupt sustainable adaptive strategies or livelihood systems, and which policies reinforce such strategies and systems.

Joy writes:

> Policy analysis should focus on people and communities, even though the policies that need analysis are all too commonly determined independently by particular (sectoral) ministries. Needed actions are likely to be multi-sectoral; in other words, they will require the engagement of several agencies.

What are some of the tools and methodologies that can be employed to set this mechanism for good governance in motion?

- computer simulations of the systems that generate marginalization
- databases
- seminars
- workshops
- consultations
- desk reviews
- participatory assessments
- planning and implementation

- key informants
- referenda
- dialogues/consultations
- comparative studies
- policy inventories
- gender analyses.

In addition, synergies between traditional knowledge and contemporary knowledge need to be promoted, while maintaining the primacy of the people's knowledge, skills, and experience.
Possible strategies for promoting good governance include:

- devolution of decision-making from top to bottom
- civic education
- gender sensitization
- the advocacy of values, principles, and processes

Structures identified where such strategies can be launched include national, local, and civil society organizations and institutions. The process required to accomplish such changes must be built on:

- consultation
- training
- awareness
- gender sensitivity

As Joy says, "The specific skills required to undertake the tasks demanded by new roles should be the basis for the most explicit training programs."

Screening policies to assess contributions to sustainable livelihoods involves:

- an analysis of adaptive strategies and continued practices
- desk reviews, comparative studies, and inventories of the polices themselves
- dialogue both with policy-makers and with those affected by the policies
- gender-sensitive analysis of policies and their effects

Advocacy strategies needed to achieve the governance and policy shifts required include:

- widespread access to information and communication channels,
- effective public service
- political tolerance
- mechanisms that can effectively:
  - fight crime and violence
  - stamp out mafias
  - establish law and order
  - promote an atmosphere of trust and generally accepted standards of conduct

Governance and the SL approach

Since good governance is crucial to poverty eradication, the SL approach needs to be applied at all levels—community, regional or district, and national—in order to promote good governance by cultivating a coherent public demand for it.

This process seeks to foster ownership at the grassroots level, and to provide the added value of the development of human capital that is necessary if citizens are to participate meaningfully in self-empowered action. The process creates an enabling environment for people to participate, in order to empower them to take control of their own development and to build their capacity to do so. As Joy says,

> Grassroots self-help activity needs to be integral with systemic strategies to address trends in marginalization and macro policy reviews. Livelihoods issues cannot be effectively tackled at the grassroots level alone.

One of the themes of the SL approach is the linkage, interdependence, or synergy between the micro and the macro, and the important benefits for development that this synergy can produce. When contemporary knowledge is applied to enhance traditional expertise, for example, added value is achieved. Joy explains,

> A linking of "downstream" livelihood programs with "upstream" programs to develop capacity for livelihood policy management should provide for mutually reinforcing efforts. Both are essential, and one without the other will prove ineffective.

Dominico Nkhuwa, son of the chief in Nyamawende, Malawi, clearly articulates his understanding:

With the change of our government to democracy, we should not misunderstand the concept. Democracy does not mean we should be sitting idle. It means we should be independent and self-reliant.

And Kristine Jones, PAPSL Advisor to the National Economic Council, Malawi, adds,

People are used to being told what to do. In the past the central government thought up good policies or bad policies and imposed them. What the SL program is trying to do is turn that around so that policy is informed by people on the ground, by rural communities.

Identifying bad policies and "perverse subsidies" and lobbying to change them is the final (though by no means sequentially the last) step of the SL process.

A central idea of the SL approach is that the process of democratization will increasingly enable local people and the organizations that represent them to serve as "watchdogs" over policies at the macro level that affect livelihoods at the micro level. Such grassroots advocates will increasingly be able to "lobby" policy-makers to design policies aimed at making livelihoods more sustainable and more productive, rather than the reverse.

Kristine Jones comments,

People do not realize that their government is accountable to them, that they can do planning for themselves. The Sustainable Livelihoods approach is very exciting because we're trying to open up that avenue for people.

If civic education leads to an improved awareness in people of how they relate to other members of the community—to society, to local government, and to the state—then that reflects very well in synergy with economic efficiency and environmental resilience. It brings in the element of social equity. People are aware of their rights and privileges and their entitlements. These are the building blocks of sustainable livelihoods.

B. T. Costantinos says:

We are using the tools of strategic planning and management for administrative coordination, and we are using multi-track communications to ensure that there is a smooth flow of information among the different activities that are being implemented. So already the synergy is being created while the building blocks are in progress. Sustainable livelihoods are an organic output of this synergy.

Communication is crucial

One of the essential aspects of good governance is communication: a free press, access to information, and channels through which people at all levels can communicate with one another. As Terence Jones says:

> We are trying to devolve government responsibilities to the district level so that government is closer to the people and more responsive, and responsible, to the people. This approach, from what we have seen so far, generates effective demand from the communities and empowers them to access resources available from government and NGOs and others. It is a nice combination of trying to make government closer to the people from the top, and building the demand from the bottom, and hoping the two will work effectively together.

The SL program is also working to set up multi-track communications systems that identify a variety of ways in which the various actors in development can communicate most successfully with each other. For example:

- UNESCO is supporting an experiment with community radio to enable communities to produce useful programming for communicating among themselves about issues and problems.
- Plays and musical productions are being successfully used to convey messages.
- Plans are in the works to train journalists based in rural areas to interview community members in order to produce programs that can be aired on the radio for discussion with policy-makers.

Sustainable livelihoods are a basic human right

If society is an ecosystem, the right to a sustainable livelihood and the dignity this right confers on everyone are essential to society's survival. Upholding this right is the collective responsibility of all strata of society, especially government. As Joy puts it:

The right is not simply to a livelihood, it is the right not to be marginalized. It is a very different way of looking at things. It is not simply protecting the rights of others, it is recognizing that their dignity has to be preserved by us, by society as a whole.

Conversely, while society is responsible for upholding the rights and dignity of the individual, the individual is also responsible to society. Joy continues:

> It is an attitude that goes back to the Kennedy quote: "Ask not what your country can do for you; ask what you can do for your country." It takes you away from the welfare state attitude, which is based on the social distance between the haves and the have-nots. This results in demeaning charity towards the have-nots, who are seen as statistics rather than as persons in communities.

If the right to a sustainable livelihood is a basic human right that is being recognized more and more around the world, upholding this right is the business of international agencies and development NGOs as they work to eradicate poverty and build capacity for good governance.

> Governance under the SL approach establishes an environment that helps release people's creativity. Then they can rise like hot air balloons. Government policies should not be a ceiling to their aspirations. They should not create obstacles for people to bump their heads against, preventing them from going further. Governance and policy at the macro level should create the very space through which people can soar.

Resources

A number of other documents that analyze and explain the Sustainable Livelihoods concept also exist in print format and at web sites. These include:

Printed materials

- Rennie, Keith, and Naresh C. Singh. *Participatory Research for Sustainable Livelihoods: A Guidebook for Field Projects.* Manitoba, Canada: International Institute for Sustainable Development, 1996.
- Singh, Naresh C., and Perpetua Kalala. *Adaptive Strategies and Sustainable Livelihoods: Community and Policy Studies for Burkino Faso, Ethiopia, Kenya, South Africa, and Zimbabwe.* Manitoba, Canada: The International Institute for Sustainable Development, 1995.
- Government of Malawi/UNDP. *Participatory Assessment, Planning, and Implementation for Sustainable Livelihoods.* Lilongwe, Malawi: UNDP Malawi, 1998.
- In Malawi, as part of the government's Sustainable Livelihoods program, a multi-track communications system is being set up. It will describe technologies that have been applied successfully in the local context, with simple instructions on how such technologies can be implemented. "The system will be used for accessing information about new technologies and for learning about experiences with technology in other districts," says UNDP resident representative Terence Jones.

Web sites

- Development Alternatives in India has set up a network (http://www.ecouncil.ac.cr/devalt/) that can connect users to the many databases of ENVIS, India's Ministry of Environment and Forests Department of Science and Technology.

- The Society for Research and Initiatives for Sustainable Technologies and Institutions (SRISTI) is a large network that reaches seventy-five countries. The SRISTI-Honey Bee network of grassroots innovators and inventions (http://www.iimahd.ernet.in/~anilg/sristi/sristi.htm or http://csf.colorado.edu/sristi) lists, among other things, local institutions initiated and governed by local people that are involved in natural resource management.

- The United Nations Development Programme's web page provides links to several papers regarding sustainable livelihoods (http://www.undp.org/sl).

- The British aid agency DFID now has the most rapidly expanding and comprehensive web site on sustainable livelihoods (http://www.livelihoods.org).

About the Authors

Kristin **Helmore** has covered development issues for nearly twenty years, reporting from Africa, Asia, and Latin America. Her articles in *The Christian Science Monitor* have garnered numerous awards, including the Overseas Press Club Award, the Sigma Delta Chi Award in Journalism, the Population Institute's Global Media Award, and the President's End Hunger Award. Helmore has authored a book analyzing development strategies for Christian Children's Fund and edited a magazine, *African Farmer*, for the Hunger Project. She has conducted mid-career training programs for journalists in Madagascar and Nigeria for the United States Information Service and is currently under contract as a writer with UNDP's Capacity 21 Programme.

Naresh **C. Singh**, Ph.D., is Principal Adviser on Poverty and Sustainable Livelihoods, Bureau for Development Policy, UNDP, New York. He is also visiting professor at Boston University (USA) and the University of Waterloo (Canada). He was instrumental in developing the ideas contained in this book, first at the International Institute for Sustainable Development (in Canada) and then at UNDP. He has worked in over forty countries around the world and published widely on the environment, poverty, and sustainable livelihoods.

About the United Nations Development Programme (UNDP)

The United Nations Development Programme is the UN's largest source of grants for development cooperation. Its funding is from voluntary contributions of member states of the United Nations and affiliated agencies. A network of 132 country offices and programs in more than 170 countries and territories help people to help themselves. In each of these countries the UNDP resident representative normally also serves as the resident coordinator of operational activities for development of the UN system as a whole. This can include humanitarian as well as development assistance.

UNDP's main priority is poverty eradication. Its work also focuses on the closely linked goals of environmental regeneration, the creation of sustainable livelihoods, and the empowerment of women. Programs for good governance and peace building create a climate for progress in these areas. Country and regional programs draw on the expertise of developing country nationals and nongovernmental organizations, the specialized agencies of the UN system, and research institutes. Seventy-five percent of all UNDP-supported projects are implemented by local organizations.

Ninety percent of UNDP's core program is focused on 66 countries that are home to 90 percent of the world's extremely poor. UNDP is a hands-on organization with 85 percent of its staff in the countries that it supports.

Index